LOVE AND SEX AND GROWING UP

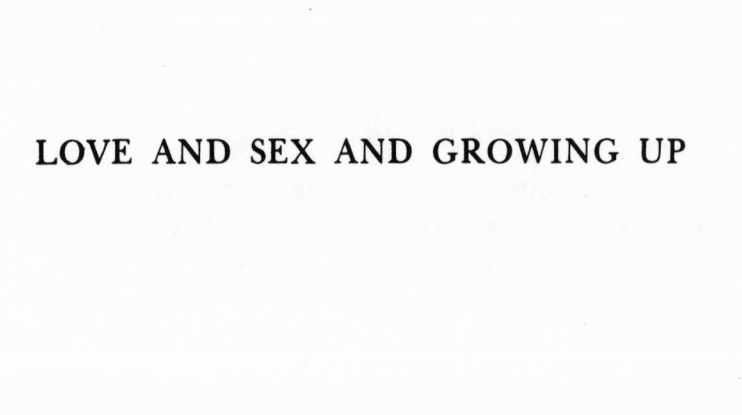

Love and Sex and Growing Up

UPDATED EDITION

Corinne Benson Johnson
Eric W. Johnson

Illustrations by Visa-Direction Studio, Inc.

Foreword by Louise Bates Ames

J. B. LIPPINCOTT COMPANY
Philadelphia   New York

U.S. Library of Congress Cataloging in Publication Data

Johnson, Corinne B
  Love and sex and growing up.

  First ed. (1970) by E. W. Johnson and C. B. Johnson.
  Includes index.
  SUMMARY: Describes the process of human reproduction
from fertilization to birth and discusses growth and
sexual maturation.
  1. Sex instruction for children. [1. Sex instruction
for children] I. Johnson, Eric W., joint author.
II. Visa-Direction Studio. III. Title.
HQ53.J6 1977   612.6   77-22462
ISBN-0-397-31768-9

UPDATED EDITION 1977

2 4 6 8 9 7 5 3 1

FOREWORD

Now that sex education has become such a *cause célèbre,* there is a greater need than ever for good sound books on the subject, books that will be clear, factual, detailed, and specific without being overly provocative or permissive.

Love and Sex and Growing Up is such a book, one which children will find both interesting and informative and one which most reasonable parents can go along with comfortably. Although it is fully frank and specific in its necessarily detailed explanation of sexual forms and functions, it places sexual behavior squarely within a family setting. This book provides a good strong step toward the understanding of the fundamentals of sexual behavior which every child must have.

Many parents who know quite definitely what they think about most burning school issues are currently somewhat confused between the extreme right point of view that there should be *no* sex education in our schools, the middle-of-the-road approach which urges a reasonable amount of sex information, and the far-left position that sex education at home or elsewhere should be permissive and exploratory.

The present volume seems to me to provide the sensible middle-of-the-road approach. Like its distinguished companion *Love and Sex in Plain Language*, this book gives needed information, this time for the pre-teen. It gives this information clearly and unambiguously, but it does not give it with any license for indulgence.

There are admittedly many available books on sex education for children of all ages. Some of the things that make this one different and specially noteworthy are:

It is, as the authors promise, more complete, frank, and detailed than most sex books for young children, and it is one of the few addressed squarely to the ten- to twelve-year-old.

It discusses boy-girl differences in a concrete and unconfusing way, and gives good and needed information about the changes that will take place in their own bodies in the next few years. In addition to providing many important facts of life, it tells the child reader how far along he himself has come toward the important goal of being grown up. And it gives a clear, fair summary of what heredity does and does not determine.

As every good book on sex should do, it discusses what sex and sexuality mean in the total context of family life and it frankly comments on the need for family planning and concern about population growth. It also gives a most realistic chapter on marriage, discussing some of its pleasures and some of its problems.

An important bonus is the dynamic section about

"Families"—the story of how man came to exist and how families came into being in the first place. And to show that man does not stand alone, there is a clear and most interesting summary of the way reproduction takes place in different kinds of plants and in animals other than man—from the simplest to the most complex.

This is a book which I believe most parents will accept for their children, and which most ten- to twelve-year-olds will find informative, interesting, and helpful.

Louise Bates Ames, Co-Director
Gesell Institute of Child Development

PREFACE

TO PARENTS AND TEACHERS

Between the time when boys and girls have learned to read well and the time when they reach puberty, there is a period, ideally of several years, during which they are curious about the facts of sex and love, a period when they are able to absorb, and enjoy absorbing, a lot of information. This book is written to be read by boys and girls during this period.

"Why tell them about sex and all those things so soon?" many may ask. "Why not wait until they are ready?" It is our view, based on our own experience with children and our discussion with many parents, that children *are* ready for sex information well before puberty. Their minds are able, and they are eager for facts. If we do not provide them with good, sound information, plainly and simply expressed, they will find their information elsewhere, and it probably will not be good, sound, or clear, although it may be simple.

Most of the children we know, by age seven or eight, know "where babies come from"—from men and

9

women mating. But they also "know" a lot of wrong "facts," and their information is usually badly out of perspective and out of context. Our sex-preoccupied society does not provide the young (or the old for that matter) with a balanced view of the development of human sexuality, or the possibilities for its expression, as an enriching and all-pervading aspect of human life. But such a balanced view is needed if people are to make sound choices and sound decisions about their behavior.

So we have written this book. It is written for children, in simple prose, but it is more complete than are other books written for young children. We start with what boys and girls know they want to know—the physical facts. We explain the sexual geography of men and women; we explain what sexual intercourse is, completely enough, we hope, to counteract distortions in children's minds which may lead to morbid (as distinguished from healthy) curiosity and even to fear; we describe the process of gestation and birth.

Having given our readers the facts they know they want, we then discuss what sex and sexuality mean in the context of human life. We discuss growing up, from babyhood to adulthood. We tell our readers that sex is a satisfaction and a pleasure, but only one of many. We discuss parents and marriage, and also people who are not married. We deal briefly with family planning and put it in the context of the world's population growth. We discuss some problems connected with sex. We try to explain, quite simply, the many

10

kinds of love: love of self, love of friends, love of comrades, brotherly love, and sexual love.

That ends Part I. It may be as much of the book as many children will want to read. But we feel that family and family life are so important that we have provided a short section, Part II, on families. It tells how man came to live in families and then describes two family systems quite different from ours, the Iroquois and the Japanese.

In nature there are, of course, many ways of reproduction, some quite like, some quite unlike, the human way. Information about these other ways of reproduction is of great interest to many boys and girls, and so we have included Part III to tell about reproduction in fish, frogs, butterflies, and birds; in mammals; and in plants.

At the very end of the book are questions and answers. They provide some more-detailed information on special subjects that interest many boys and girls. The questions and answers are keyed into the main part of the book.

How the Book May Be Used

We have written the book with the individual boy or girl reader in mind, the young person who wants to know and is ready to find out through the private experience of reading a book. However, many parts of the book will doubtless raise questions in the mind of

11

the young reader, and it will be helpful to him if his parents and teachers have also read the book and are ready to discuss it with him.

Also, the book can well be used in the classroom, either occasionally as interest develops, or as the basis for an organized series of lesson-discussions.

No book can, or should try to, provide sex education complete in one volume. Even more important than book-reading is discussion with mature, enlightened people, and discussion with one's peers. Sex education must be continuous, and discussion of the sexual aspects of life must take place again and again, in different situations and with different people. We hope that this book will provide the material for such education and the occasion for many such discussions.

Corinne Benson Johnson
Eric W. Johnson

ACKNOWLEDGMENTS

A number of people have read the manuscript of this book and given suggestions for corrections and improvements. We credit them with much that is good in the text. For any shortcomings that remain, the responsibility is entirely ours.

Our thanks go to the following:

Mrs. Louise Bates Ames, New Haven, Co-Director, Gesell Institute of Child Development.

John Boles, Princeton, N.J., Production Editor, *Textile Research Journal;* former teacher of biology, Germantown Friends School; former editor, *Not Man Apart,* Friends of the Earth.

Joseph M. Cadbury, Waldoboro, Maine, former teacher of science, Germantown Friends School elementary grades.

Mary S. Calderone, M.D., M.P.H., New York, President, Sex Information and Education Council of the United States (SIECUS).

John B. Emerson, Philadelphia, Director of Admissions and teacher of religious studies, Germantown Friends School.

Steven R. Homel, M.D., Philadelphia, pediatrician, Jefferson Hospital; Director, Center for Health Education; special consultant in sex education for school districts throughout the United States; author, *Sex Education in Perspective,* Pennsylvania Department of Education.

S. Leon Israel, M.D., Philadelphia, late Professor of Obstetrics and Gynecology, School of Medicine, University of Pennsylvania; Director, Department of Obstetrics and Gynecology, Pennsylvania Hospital.

John Keats, Philadelphia, author of books and articles of social criticism; and Margaret Bodine Keats.

Dr. Eleanore Braun Luckey, Salt Lake City, Professor and Chairman, Family and Consumer Studies, the University of Utah.

David C. McClelland, Cambridge, Mass., Professor of Psychology, Department of Social Relations, Harvard University; author of books in his field; and Mary Warner McClelland.

Norval D. Reece, Harrisburg, Pa., Pennsylvania Secretary of Commerce; and Ann Benson Reece.

C.B.J.
E.W.J.

CONTENTS

PART 2
FAMILIES: SOME HISTORY
AND SOME DIFFERENCES

PART 3
OTHER WAYS OF REPRODUCING:
ANIMALS AND PLANTS

PART I

LOVE AND SEX AND
GROWING UP

CHAPTER 1

WHAT THIS BOOK IS ABOUT

This book is about love, sex, babies, marriage, and families. It is about male and female. It tells about people—and also something about plants and animals. But mainly it is about people.

You are probably curious about these things, especially about people. Good, for a person who wants to know is a person who is growing and learning as he should.

You have undoubtedly heard the word *sex*. You know that a person's sex is either male or female. A boy or man belongs to the male sex. A girl or woman belongs to the female sex.

But the word sex means much more than that. It means the act by which a man and woman come together and start babies. This is called the sex act. Sex also means the whole relationship between men and women.

A person is likely to be called *sexy* if he or she has a body that attracts others and if he or she acts in a way that attracts others physically—to his or her body. (Older boys may whistle at or sigh over a sexy girl.

Older girls may do the same over a sexy boy.) Being sexy is only one kind of attraction between males and females, but it is a very strong one.

Sex can also mean the feelings of pleasure you can have in your own body as you grow up.

If you are in elementary school you are a long way from being a baby, but you are not yet an adult. From this book you can learn how far along you yourself have come toward being grown up. When you are further grown you will understand better the strong feelings that love and sex can make between men and women.

In Part I of the book, we begin by explaining what makes one person a woman, and what makes another person a man. Then we describe how a woman and a man come together to start a new life growing and how that life becomes a baby and is born. We talk about the growth of a child. We talk about other meanings of sex. We talk about love, marriage, and families.

In Part II of the book, we talk more about families and how they came to be. In Part III, we describe how animals and plants reproduce themselves. At the very end of the book, we answer some of the questions you may still want to ask.

CHAPTER 2

A WOMAN

Living things have a beginning and an end. They start life, they grow, they go on living, and they die. While they are alive, they can produce other living things like themselves—they can *re*produce. If living things did not reproduce, their form of life would not continue after their deaths. They would die out—become *extinct*.

Living things have various ways of reproducing. Human beings reproduce *sexually*. This means that both a woman and a man—a female and a male— are needed to produce a new human being. Both contribute a part to the new life.

In Figure 1 you see a drawing of parts of a woman's body. These are the parts that have to do with making babies. They are called her *sex organs*.

Inside her body, the woman has cells which can grow into babies. These female sex cells, or eggs, are stored in her *ovaries*. The two, oval-shaped ovaries are each an inch or two long. They are in the lowest part of the woman's abdomen or belly, one on each side.

When a girl baby is born, there are about 400,000

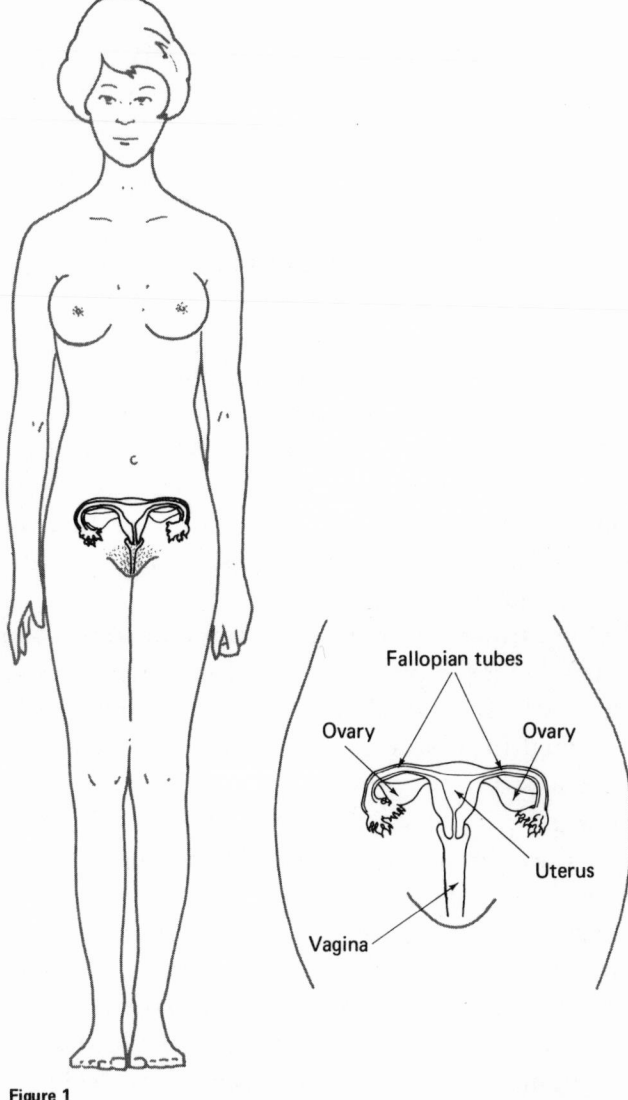

Fallopian tubes

Ovary

Ovary

Uterus

Vagina

Figure 1

eggs already in her ovaries, many many more than she will ever need. These are not fully grown eggs. Something starts to happen to the eggs when the girl is from ten to sixteen years old. Once about every 28 days one egg ripens—becomes fully grown. This monthly ripening goes on until a woman is forty-five to fifty.

A ripe egg is very small. Two hundred side by side would make a row only an inch long. Yet each egg carries inside it enough food to keep it alive for a few days, in case it is to grow into a baby.

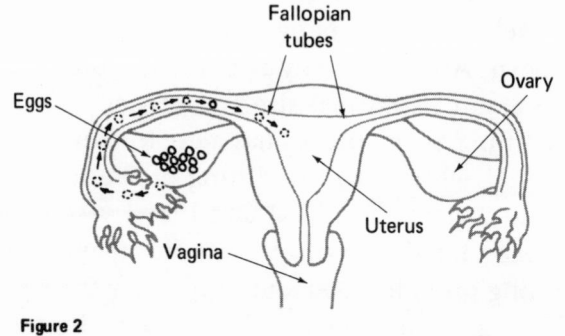

Figure 2

The ripe egg is pushed out of the side of the ovary with a little burst. (Some women feel a slight pain when this happens.) The egg is caught in the end of the *fallopian tube* that is nearby (see Figure 2). The egg has no way of moving itself. But inside each of the tubes are small hairs which wave in one direction. They move the egg slowly down the tube for three or four days.

The woman cannot start a baby by herself. The man must contribute, too. A male sex cell, or *sperm,* has to

23

join with the woman's egg in the tube in order to start a new life growing. If a sperm joins the egg, the egg is *fertilized*. It begins immediately to grow into a baby. This growing takes about nine months in all.

The fertilized egg is moved on down the tube to the place where it can live while it is growing into a baby. This place is called the *uterus* or *womb*. It is just about in the middle of the woman's body. It is the size and shape of a pear, stem down.

The uterus is an amazing organ. It is the home for the unborn baby. It also gives it food, warmth, and protection. It stretches as the baby grows. It has muscles to help push the baby out when it is time for it to be born. After the baby is born, the uterus shrinks back to about its normal size and shape.

The lining of the uterus has a great many blood vessels in it. Each month, the lining of the uterus grows thicker and richer in blood and blood vessels. This is to be ready for the fertilized egg that may be coming. The lining provides food and oxygen for the egg.

If the egg is not fertilized, the extra lining is not needed. Then, ten to fourteen days after the egg leaves the ovary, this lining gradually breaks up. It is emptied out through a passage that opens between the woman's legs. This passage is called the *vagina,* and it is about three inches long (see Figure 3). The woman may feel cramps in her uterus when this happens, or she may not feel any pain at all.

This monthly flow of the lining is called *menstruation*. It lasts from three to seven days. A woman says she is "having her period" when she is menstruating.

She wears a pad between her legs or a tampon in her vagina to collect the flow of menstruation. She changes the pad or tampon for a clean one when it is needed, throwing the used one away. After menstruation stops, another egg begins to ripen in one of the ovaries. The lining of the uterus begins again to grow richer, ready for the next egg, in a new *monthly cycle*.

But if the egg has been fertilized and has started to grow in the uterus, then there is no menstruation. Then no new egg comes from the ovaries until after the baby is born.

Before   During   After

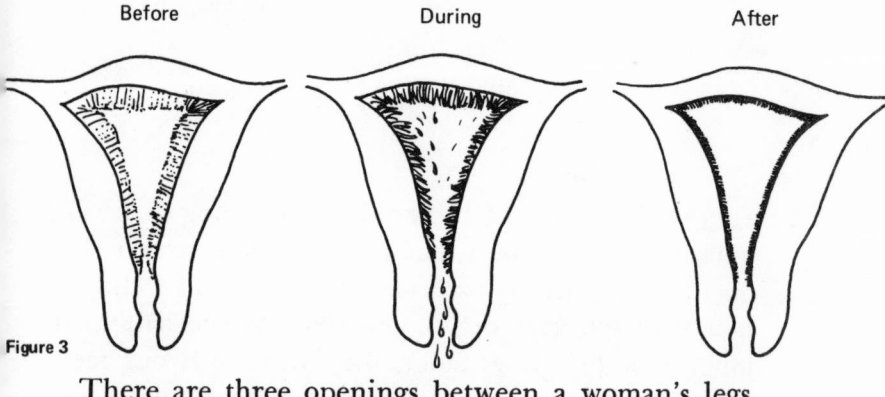

Figure 3

There are three openings between a woman's legs (see Figure 4). The front one is for passing water, or urine. It is called the *urethra*. The middle one is the opening of the vagina. The back one is for bowel movements and is called the *anus*.

The vagina has several uses. It is a passage for menstrual flow. It stretches to let a baby through as it is born. It is the place where sperms are placed by the man, one of which may fertilize the egg.

The sex organs on the surface of the woman's body

25

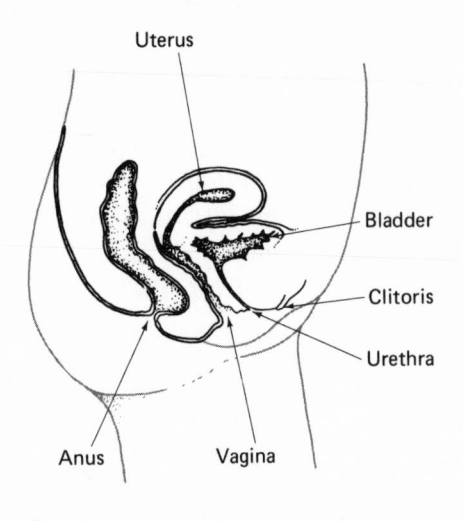

Uterus

Bladder

Clitoris

Urethra

Anus

Vagina

Figure 4

are called her *genitals*. They are the opening of the vagina, the folds of skin that surround and protect this opening, and the *clitoris* (see Figure 4). The clitoris is a very sensitive organ, one-sixth to one-half inch long. As a girl grows older, she will have strong feelings of sex pleasure in her clitoris. But the clitoris is not necessary for reproduction.

CHAPTER 3

A MAN

In Figure 5, you see a drawing of the sex organs of a man. The man's sex cells, or *sperms,* are made by two organs. The organs are about the same size and shape as a woman's ovaries. They are the man's *testicles.* The testicles are carried outside the man's body rather than in it. They are in a pouch of skin that hangs between his legs. This pouch is called the *scrotum.*Q1 *

The man's sex cell looks like a very small tadpole (see Figure 6). The body of the "tadpole" is the reproductive cell. The tail makes the sperm swim. It wriggles.

The sperm is different from the woman's egg in several ways. It does not carry any food within itself. Therefore, it is much smaller. One hundred thousand sperms would fit in the same space as one egg. The sperm can move itself along by lashing its tail. The egg cannot move itself at all. New sperms are always being

*Q1: This sign means that there is more information about the testicles and scrotum in the question and answer section of the book. See page 113.

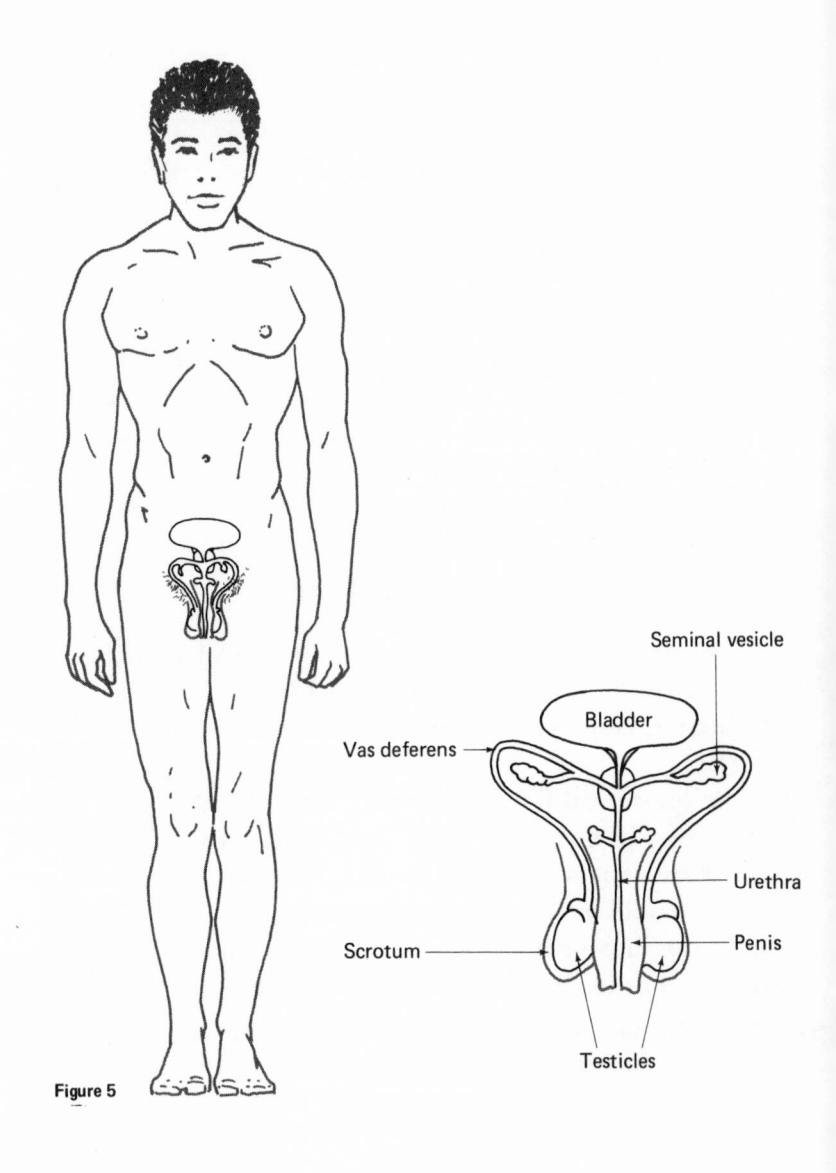

Seminal vesicle

Bladder

Vas deferens

Urethra

Scrotum

Penis

Testicles

Figure 5

made in a man's testicles. A woman's ovaries do not make any new eggs. They store the eggs she already had when she was born.

From the testicles, the sperms move into a tube called the *vas deferens*. It leads the sperms up into the man's body from the scrotum.

After they go through the vas deferens, the sperms mix with a fluid which helps keep them alive and vigorous. The mixture of sperms and fluid is called *semen*. It is stored in two sacs, the *seminal vesicles* (see

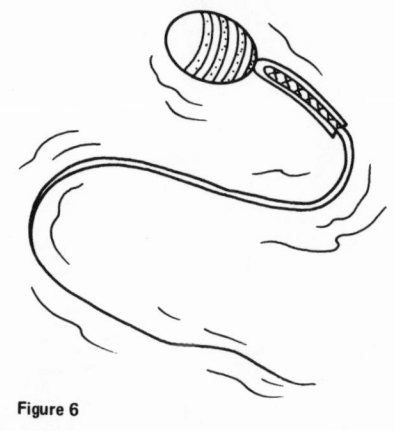

Figure 6

Figure 5). The semen passes out of the man's body through the same tube that goes from his *bladder* down through his penis. This tube is the man's *urethra*. (The bladder is where urine is stored.)

The man's most obvious sex organs are his *penis* and scrotum. These are his genitals. The penis is three to four inches long. It is somewhat thicker than the man's thumb. It hangs down from his groin between his legs, in front of his scrotum. The man urinates through his

29

penis. He also uses his penis to put semen inside the woman's vagina.

Semen and urine can never mix together because a special valve keeps them from passing out of the man's body at the same time.

When a boy is born, the end of his penis is covered by a fold of skin. This is his *foreskin*. Shortly after his birth, the baby's foreskin may be cut off by a doctor. This is a very simple operation. It is called *circumcision*. Circumcision is usually done because it makes it

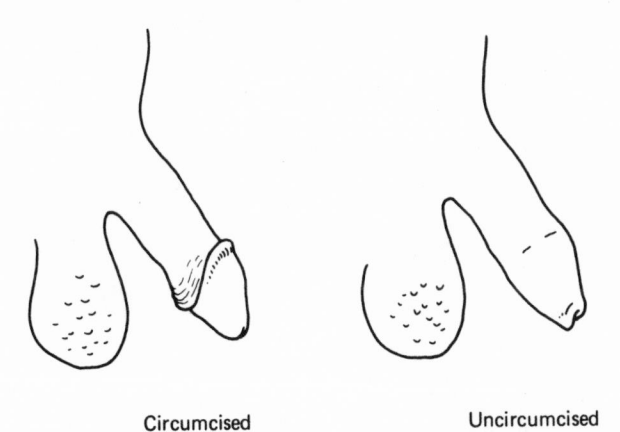

Circumcised   Uncircumcised

Figure 7

easier to keep the penis clean. Among Jews it is done also for religious reasons. Figure 7 shows a circumcised penis and an uncircumcised one.

CHAPTER 4

HOW A BABY STARTS GROWING

A new human life starts when one of a man's sperms joins a woman's egg. This can happen when a man and a woman *mate* with each other. Usually they mate in bed. They get ready for mating in various ways—by speaking lovingly to each other, by hugging and kissing. When the man is ready, his penis, which is usually limp and hangs down between his legs, has become enlarged and stiff. It points outward from his body. This is called an *erection*. When the woman is ready, her vagina has become soft and moist so that it can receive the man's penis easily.

The man then puts his penis into the woman's vagina. The man and the woman move back and forth together, and after a time the penis spurts about a teaspoonful of semen into the woman's vagina.[22] The sperms can then swim to meet the egg (see Figure 8). This mating of man and woman is called *sexual intercourse*.

The spurting out of semen—*ejaculation*—is the climax of sexual intercourse for a man. The woman has a climax, too. The walls of her vagina contract sev-

31

eral times, but there is no sudden discharge of fluid. In both men and women, the climax gives great pleasure.

Sexual intercourse is a private experience that a man and a woman share. It can make them feel very close, besides serving as the way to bring the sperm to the egg so that a new life can start.

A woman produces one ripe egg, about once a month. The egg can live only for about half a day, if it is not fertilized. A sperm can live inside the woman's body for two to three days. Live sperms must be in the woman's tube when a live ripe egg is there also, if a new life is to start. So a baby will not always

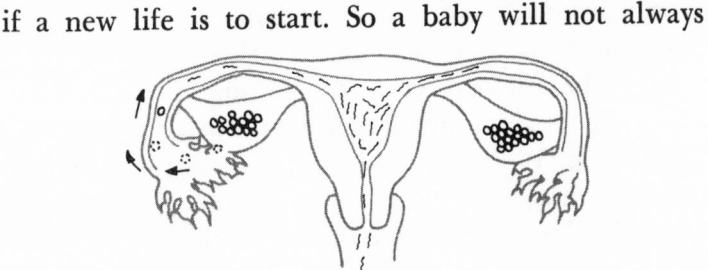

Figure 8

be started—*conceived*—as a result of sexual intercourse.

When the egg and a sperm join, they form one cell. From this single cell a human baby will grow. At birth, the baby will be made up of millions of cells. This growth comes about by cell division (see Figure 9). The first cell divides into two cells. Then each of the new cells divides, making four. The four cells divide, making eight, and so on.

The fertilized egg, already dividing and growing, continues to be moved along the woman's tube. It reaches the uterus three or four days after the egg leaves the ovary. It settles into the uterus lining. It keeps on dividing. At first each cell is the same as all the others, but gradually the cells take on special jobs. Some cells will make the skin of the new baby. Others will make the muscles, brain, nerves, and bones. Still others will make the internal organs.

For about the first four months, the developing egg is called an *embryo*. The embryo of a human being has the beginnings of gills like a fish for a short time.

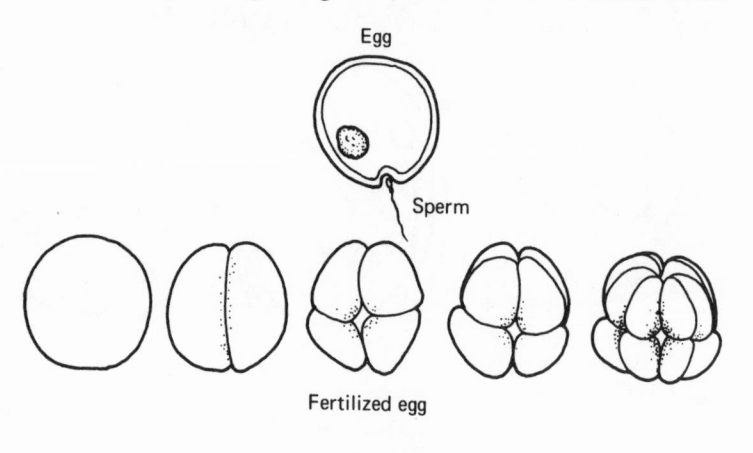

Figure 9

Later it has a tail. Figure 10 shows a human embryo one month old beside embryos of various animals. At this time, the human embryo is about a quarter of an inch long. And, as you can see, it is hard to tell apart from the others. But the human embryo soon becomes recognizable as human.

The human embryo is shown at two, three, and four months in Figure 11. You can see how it develops. At four months, the embryo is six inches long and weighs

33

a third of a pound. It can move its arms and legs. The mother can feel these movements.

From four months on, the embryo is called a *fetus*. You can see in Figure 12 how it develops. By six months the fetus looks quite a lot like a baby, except that it does not yet have any "baby fat."

A baby born *before* six months rarely survives. Its organs (which include its heart, lungs, and stomach) are not fully made. They may not be able to work properly to keep the baby alive. A baby born at six

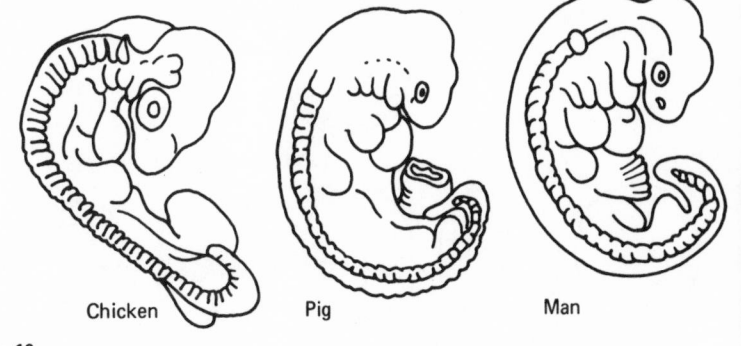

Chicken   Pig   Man

Figure 10

months has a chance to live, but it needs very good, special care. It may weigh about two pounds. If a six-months baby is born in a hospital, it is placed in an incubator (see Figure 13) until it is big and strong enough to live without special protection. The incubator keeps the baby warm and protected almost the way the uterus does. Babies born early are called *premature*. Most babies stay in the mother's uterus for the full term of nine months. They weigh about six to eight pounds when they are born.

During the time the embryo (and then the fetus) is

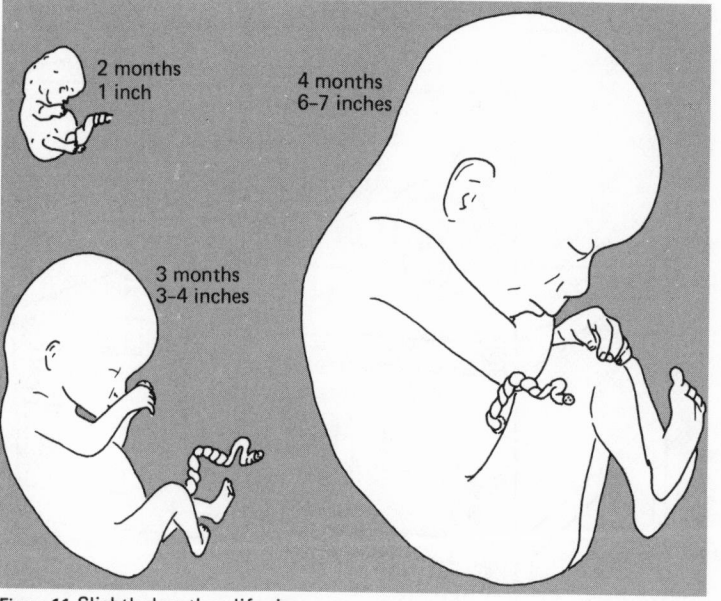

Figure 11 Slightly less than life size

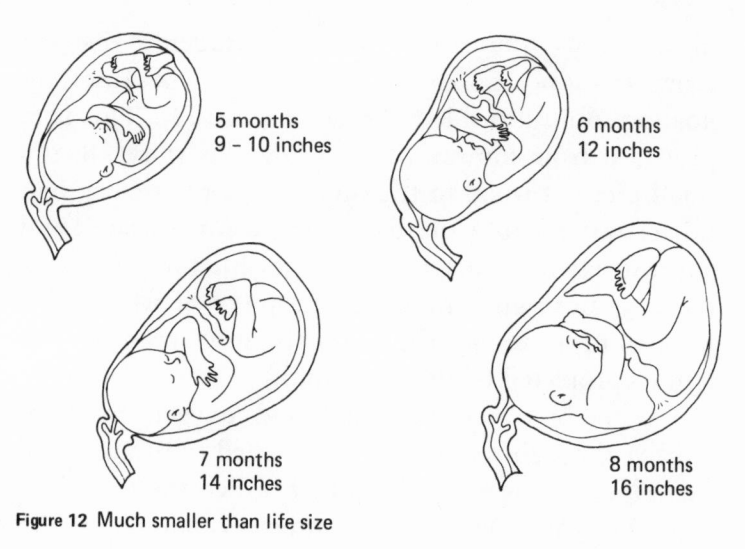

Figure 12 Much smaller than life size

35

Figure 13

in the uterus, it must have food and oxygen to live and grow. It cannot eat or breathe for itself because it is floating in fluid inside a sac (see Figure 14). This is to protect it from bumps. (To see how this works, float a small piece of wood in the middle of a plastic bag half full of water. Hold the bag at the top with one hand and hit it with the other. You can hit the outside of the bag, but you cannot hit the piece of wood. The wood is protected by the water the way an embryo or fetus is protected by its sac of fluid.)

The embryo receives food and oxygen from its mother through a sort of tube attached to its abdomen (see Figure 14 again). The tube is called the *umbilical cord*. The cord goes from the embryo's abdomen to the

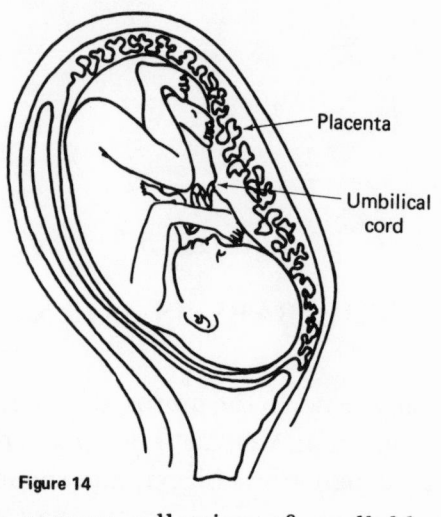

Placenta

Umbilical cord

Figure 14

placenta, a spongy collection of small blood vessels. The placenta is attached to the wall of the mother's uterus. Blood in the placenta picks up food and oxygen from the mother's blood. These go through the cord to the embryo (or fetus). Waste from the embryo goes back the other way and passes across to the mother. The blood of the mother and the blood of the embryo or fetus do not mix. The developing baby makes its own blood.

CHAPTER 5

THE BABY IS BORN

While the baby grows in the uterus, the uterus stretches to give it room. The woman is *pregnant* during this time. Her abdomen grows bigger, and she looks fatter. Her breasts grow larger. They are getting ready to give milk for the baby when it is born. (See Figure 15.)

When the time comes for the baby to be born, the mother's uterus stops stretching. Its strong muscles begin to contract. They draw together time after time in a sort of rhythm. This is hard work for the mother. It can hurt because the muscles often have to keep working hard for a long time. The contracting of the muscles is called *labor*. Labor may last anywhere from a few minutes to more than a day.

Figure 16 shows how a baby is born. Usually the baby has turned so that it is head down in the uterus. As the muscles of the mother's uterus contract, the baby breaks through the bag of waters that hold it. The neck of the uterus stretches open, and the baby's head pushes out into the vagina. The vagina also stretches to let the baby through. The baby finally comes out between its mother's legs.

Figure 15

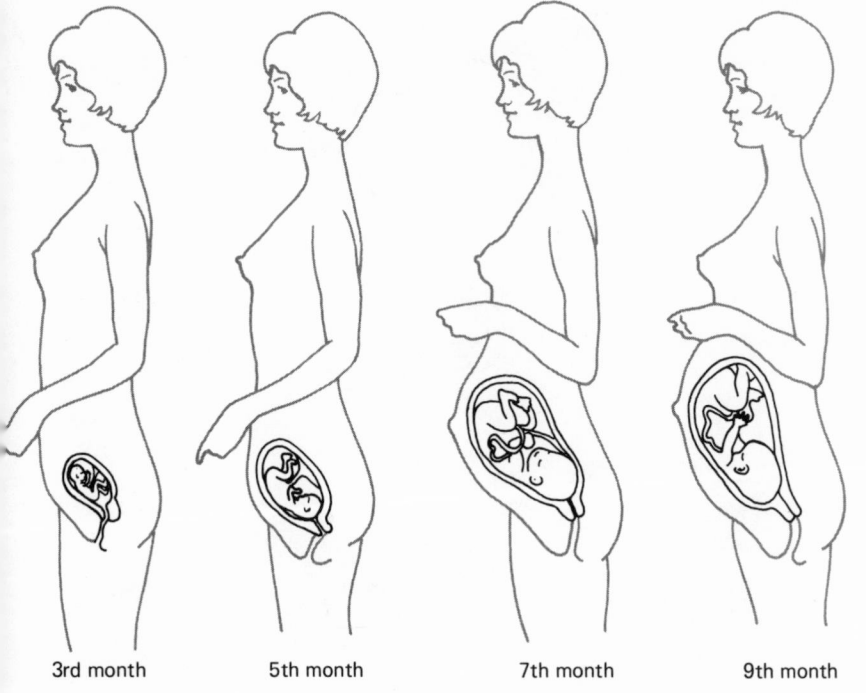

| 3rd month | 5th month | 7th month | 9th month |

After the baby's birth, the mother's uterus keeps on contracting. This is to push out the placenta and the sac that held the baby. These are called the *afterbirth,* and they are thrown away.

You remember that the fetus in its mother's uterus was not able to breathe and eat for itself. It got its food and oxygen from the mother through the umbilical cord. When the baby is born, it starts to breathe and it can suck to get food. The cord is no longer needed. Shortly after the baby is born, the cord is tied and cut by the doctor or nurse who is helping at the birth. Cutting it does not hurt the baby or the mother, because

39

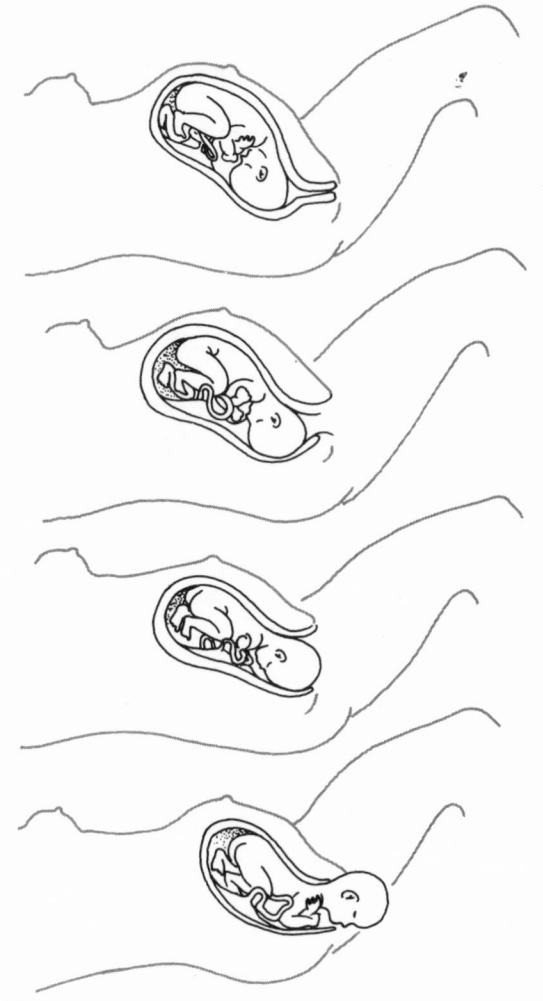

Figure 16

there are no nerves in the cord. Your *navel* or belly-button is the place where your umbilical cord was attached to you.

Brothers and sisters, and fathers and mothers, too, think of a baby as being pretty and cute. Often when they see a newborn baby for the first time they are disappointed. The baby's head may have been pushed out of shape when it was born. The baby may look red and lumpy and even angry, not at all pretty. After a few days the head goes back into shape, the skin becomes a normal color, and the baby grows used to breathing and eating independently. Then the baby begins to look more the way we think babies should look.

In this country and many others, a woman usually goes to the hospital to have her baby. At the hospital a doctor and nurses can help while the baby is being born. Also the mother can rest afterward, and can have help with the baby for a few days. At the hospital, too, a doctor checks the new baby to be sure it is healthy.

In places where there are not enough doctors and hospitals, a baby is likely to be born at home. Nurses, or women called *midwives,* who have learned a lot about the birth of babies, help the mother.

After the baby is born, the mother's breasts begin to produce milk. The newborn baby gets food at first just from sucking milk. This comes either from the mother's breasts or from a bottle. The milk given in a bottle usually is cow's milk with other things added to make it as much like mother's milk as possible. This is called *formula.*

After the baby's birth, the mother's abdomen is suddenly much smaller. She looks about the way she did before she was pregnant. Her breasts may be larger because they are providing milk for the baby. It takes about six weeks for her uterus to go all the way back to its normal shape and size.

CHAPTER 6

WHAT YOU GET FROM YOUR MOTHER AND YOUR FATHER

Who will the new baby look like? In a family, one child may look a lot like the mother, another child may look more like the father. Some children are a mixture of both. Perhaps you have been told that you have your mother's eyes, your father's mouth. The resemblance may go farther back, and a child may look or even act like a grandparent, an aunt, or an uncle.

What is passed on to you from your mother and your father is called your *heredity*. It includes what your body will look like—whether you will be short or tall, light- or heavy-boned. Heredity decides your eye color, your skin and hair color, and whether you will have straight or curly hair. What is passed on to you also may include some of your talents—for music, sports, art, numbers, words, work with your hands, for example.

But heredity does not decide everything. Exactly how tall or heavy you will be depends partly on what kind of food, rest, and health care you have. Heredity does not decide what you will do with your talents and

42

abilities, either. That depends a great deal on what happens to you after you are born. It depends on whether you are close to other people with the same talents and interests who can encourage you. It depends on how hard you try, on how good your teachers and coaches are, on how much time you can spend learning, and on how good a learner you are.

Let us see how heredity works. Very, very small parts of the egg cell and the sperm cell decide what the heredity of the new baby will be. These are called the baby's *genes*. The baby gets half his genes from his mother and half from his father.

Each child in a family inherits different genes from its mother and different genes from its father. Which genes it receives depends on chance. This is one reason that brothers and sisters are different in many ways. The only time this is not true is in the case of some twins—two babies born at the same time.

Twins can be started in two ways. Some twins are started from one fertilized egg. The egg divides into two separate parts. Then each of these parts develops into a baby. Finally twins are born. The twins are almost exactly the same, because they have come from the same egg and the same sperm. Both inherit the same genes from their parents. They are called *identical* twins (see Figure 17).

Perhaps you know twins who look so much alike that people are confused and cannot tell which one they are talking to. Those are identical twins. Identical twins are always the same sex.

Other twins are started when there are two eggs in

the woman's tubes at about the same time. Each egg is fertilized by a separate sperm. The two fertilized eggs then grow at the same time in the mother's uterus. The two babies are born at about the same time. But they are no more alike than ordinary brothers and sisters. They have received different sets of genes from their parents. They may be the same sex or they may be boy and girl. They are called *fraternal* twins (see Figure 18).[3, 4]

Triplets, quadruplets, or quintuplets are born when three, four, or five babies have grown in the uterus at

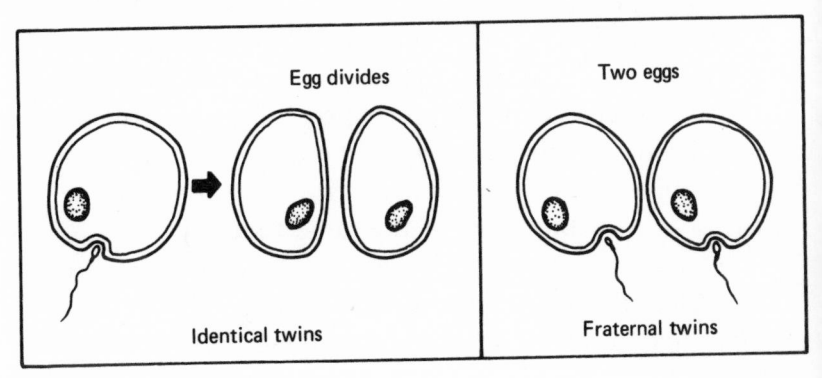

Egg divides — Two eggs

Identical twins — Fraternal twins

Figure 17

Figure 18

the same time. These brothers and sisters may be identical or fraternal. Or there may be some of each. Births of more than two babies at once are unusual.

Parents often would like to know whether their new baby will be a boy or a girl. But there is no simple way for them to find this out before the baby is born. Parents usually just have to wait. The sperm carries the gene that determines whether the baby will be a boy

44

or a girl. And it is determined at the moment the sperm joins the egg, once and for all.

A man probably has the same number of sperms with genes for girls as he has sperms with genes for boys. But that does not mean that half the children in each family will be girls and half boys. You all know families with only girls or only boys. By chance, the fertilizing sperms have always been sperms for the same sex. This could happen in any family, but most large families do have some boys and some girls.[95]

CHAPTER 7

GROWING UP: BABY TO SMALL CHILD

New babies are pretty helpless. They can sleep. They can breathe. They can move their arms and legs, they can suck, they can cry, and they can urinate and empty their bowels. They depend on their mothers for almost everything: food, warmth, cleanliness, and loving.

New babies like their stomachs to be full of milk, and they like to be warm and dry. They like to be cuddled, rocked, patted, handled. They drink milk by their own sucking. They are likely to find that sucking is fun even when they are full, that cuddling is nice even when they are warm. Babies suck their thumbs, their

45

clothes, their toys. They try every new thing in their mouths. They like to be picked up and held when they are awake.

As babies grow older, they learn many new things. One thing they learn is that they are separate people. They can tell that they are people and their mothers are other people. They can tell that toys, bed, and food are things which are not part of themselves. When babies are about one year old they learn to walk. At about two, they start to talk. They can understand what other people want. They can make others understand what they want.

When they are very young, babies take. They take food, they take love—and they give nothing back, except smiles or gurgles. When they can talk and walk, they can start to give as well as take. They like to hand things to their mothers or fathers and hear them say "Thank you." They hug their mothers or fathers to show affection the same way the parents have been showing theirs. They like the give-and-take of rough-housing. They are probably very proud of what they give and proud of being able to give.

Babies keep growing and learning. They begin to know people outside the family. They learn to play and to share. They see that other people have needs and rights, too. During the years from about three to five, children start to make friends their own age. They may go to nursery or play school.

Boys and girls around this age realize for the first time a very important thing. They realize that boys and girls are made differently. A boy may see his little sister or a girl playmate going to the bathroom, taking a bath, having diapers changed, or swimming. He sees that she has no penis and scrotum. Since up to this time he has learned only about himself, he may think there is something wrong with the little girl.

In the same way, a girl may see a boy going to the bathroom, taking a bath, having his diapers changed, or swimming. She sees that he has a penis and scrotum between his legs, things she does not have. She may wonder why she does not have them.

Both the boy and the girl learn that they are made differently because they are going to grow up to be different. They learn that is the way it is supposed to be. The boy will grow up to be a man and probably a father. His penis and scrotum are right for him. The girl is going to be a woman and probably a mother. Her vagina and other sex organs are right for her.

Infants and young children are likely to discover that handling their genitals feels good. They may touch their genitals in order to have this pleasant feeling. Some do it often, some not so often.

Small children are growing ready for school and lessons. But before school they learn a great deal, probably more than they will ever learn at school. They learn about people—about themselves and their families and their playmates. They learn about how their world works, how people are related to each other.

Children of preschool age learn that men and women marry and have families. They believe that they will want to marry, too. A little boy may decide that he wants to marry his mother when he is grown up. A little girl may decide she will marry her father. They often think their mother or father is the best person to marry. They cannot see far enough ahead to realize that they will really marry someone outside their family and probably nearer their own age. But they are learning something about what marriage is.

Boys and girls need to know a lot about the world and themselves before they go to school. They have to know how to get along with other children, how to take care of themselves in many ways, how to listen, how to sit still for a while, how to walk, talk, and do things with their hands. They learn all these things in their first four or five years, mostly at home.

CHAPTER 8

GROWING UP:
CHILD FROM SIX TO TEENS

Boys and girls turn to new things in the years from six on. They go to school. They are away from home and from their families much of the time. They are busy learning about things outside themselves most of the time. Their bodies are not changing a great deal but are growing slowly and steadily, preparing for the changes that will come in the teen years.

Up to now it has not mattered much whether playmates were girls or boys. Now, though, boys are likely to want to play with boys, girls with girls. Boys may tease girls; girls may chase boys. There may sometimes be some special boy and girl friends. But most of the time boys want to play games, start projects, or rough-house with other boys. Girls usually want to work and talk and play with other girls.

Some girls, however, prefer being with boys and playing what people think of as boys' games. They used to be called *tomboys*. These girls probably also have girl friends. Some boys are not so sports-minded as others, and they may enjoy being with girls, though they probably also have some boy friends, too.

These girls and boys are somewhat different from most of their classmates in what they like or are will-ing to do. They may feel lonely sometimes, and their classmates may tease them. But times and ideas are changing, and there are fewer and fewer activities just for boys or just for girls. Girls play on baseball teams. Boys enjoy cooking and knitting. Generally, as every-one grows up, the differences seem even less important.

Children in the elementary grades at school learn reading and writing and numbers. They learn about the sun and moon and stars, about space and astro-nauts. They learn about the earth, the sea, animals, and people. They want information. They are hungry for facts. One thing they want information about is their own and other people's bodies.

Boys and girls are likely to be very interested in learning about men's and women's bodies, from science classes or picture magazines. That is a part of growing

49

and learning—it is a natural and healthy thing to be curious and to find out about what interests you. It is ignorance that is likely to hurt you, not information. Therefore, this period from age six to ten or twelve is a time of discovery and learning. It is a time of gradual growth. It leads to the next step in growing—the step in which boys and girls become men and women.

CHAPTER 9

GROWING UP: TEEN-AGER TO ADULT

When boys and girls are between ten or eleven and fifteen or sixteen years old, their bodies begin to change quite rapidly. These changes are very important. They come at a time called *puberty*.

Let us take a boy first and see what happens to him at this time (see Figure 19). Usually when he is around thirteen or fourteen (but it can be a lot earlier or later), he begins to grow hair around and above his penis. This is called *pubic hair*. He also begins to grow more hair on his body: under his arms, on his arms and legs, sometimes on his chest and back, and finally on his face (his mustache and beard). Also, the boy's voice box grows larger. This is what makes his voice change to the deeper voice of a man (see Figure 20).

For a couple of years the boy grows taller much faster than he has grown before. His shoulders grow

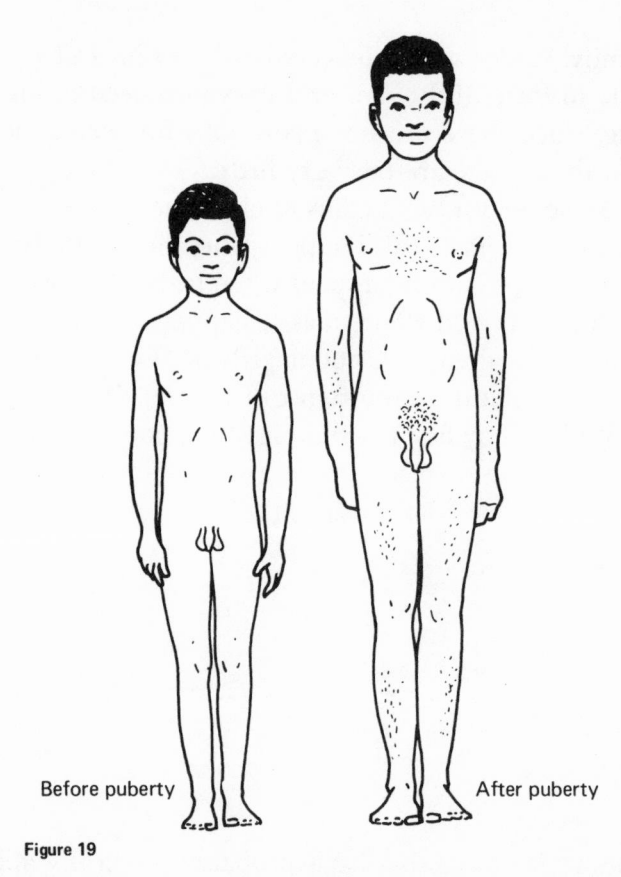

Before puberty   After puberty

Figure 19

wider, his hips and waist relatively slimmer. The features of his face—nose, mouth, chin—grow bigger and less boyish. His skin becomes oilier and he may be bothered by pimples, or *acne*.

At puberty, too, a boy's genitals become larger.[Q6] His testicles begin to make sperms. He could become the father of children even though according to the rules of our society he is not grown up enough to marry. He is probably not yet mature enough to help build a

51

family. And it would be very hard for him and a young wife to earn all the money they would need to support one, since there are not many jobs for young people and those there are pay very little.

At puberty a boy begins to ejaculate semen from his penis. Sometimes this happens when he is handling his penis. Sometimes it happens when he is in close contact with a girl. And sometimes it happens at night, often when he is dreaming about girls or sex. These night-time ejaculations are often called "wet dreams."

When a boy first ejaculates semen, no matter how he

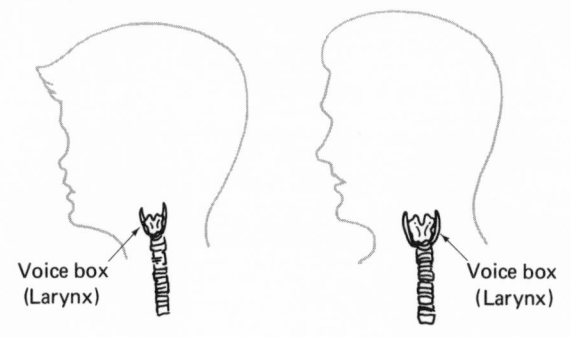

Voice box (Larynx)

Voice box (Larynx)

Figure 20

does it, it means that he is probably physically able to become a father.[Q7, 8, 9]

The time that starts with puberty and ends with adulthood is called *adolescence*. In adolescence many boys begin to be interested in girls in a new way. They like to be around girls. They want the girls to notice them and to think they are fun to be with.

Boys begin to think more about how they look. They may comb their hair and choose their clothes carefully. They may look in their mirrors frequently.

52

To their younger brothers and sisters this may seem pretty silly, but it is a sign that the adolescents are growing up.

A girl is likely to reach puberty when she is twelve or thirteen, though it may be a lot earlier or later (see Figure 21). The girl's breasts become noticeably larger. Pubic hair begins to grow around and above her genitals. Hair also grows under her arms, on her arms and legs, sometimes in a faint mustache on her upper lip. The girl's voice box grows bigger, too, giving her voice the fuller sound of a woman's, but this is not as notice-

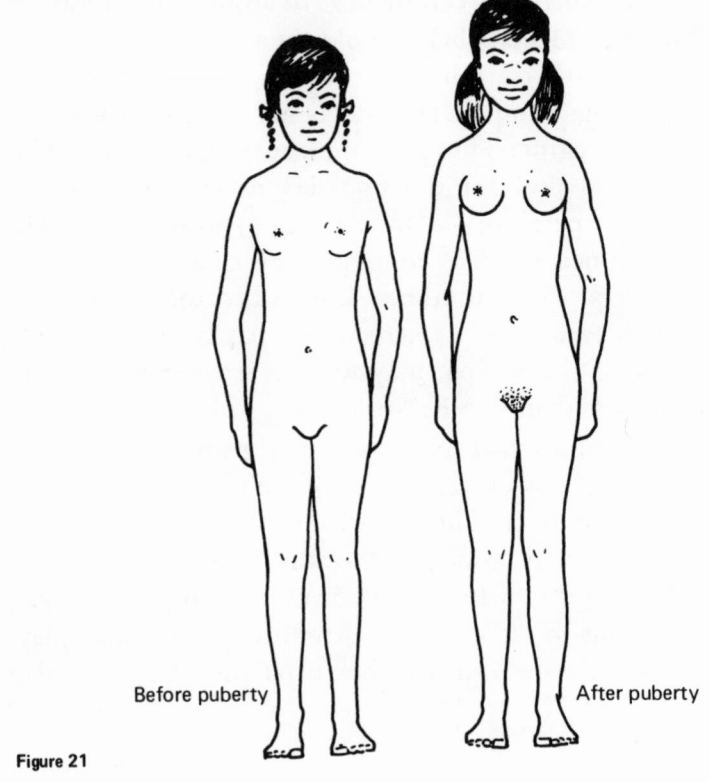

Before puberty After puberty

Figure 21

able as it is in boys. The girl's skin also becomes oilier, and she may be troubled by acne.

At puberty there are also changes in a girl's sex organs. She begins to menstruate (see page 24). Her ovaries start to produce ripe eggs, sometimes at the time she starts to menstruate, sometimes earlier, or often one or two years later.

A girl can do several things to be ready for her first menstruation. She can talk with her mother or another woman about menstruation. She can buy the supplies she will need: *sanitary pads* or *sanitary napkins* (pads that are worn between the legs to absorb the menstrual flow) and a special belt to hold them in place.

Some girls learn how to use *tampons* right from the beginning. Tampons are absorbent rolls that are worn inside the vagina. They stay in place without a belt. The menstrual flow for the first day or two may be too heavy to be absorbed by a tampon, so that a napkin may be needed, too. Some girls are not able to use a tampon as easily as others. This is because a thin piece of flesh called the hymen, which partly closes the entrance of the vagina, may leave a smaller opening in some girls than in others.[910]

Companies that make sanitary pads and tampons have free booklets telling about menstruation and how to prepare for it. There is a list of these companies and their addresses on page 120 of this book.

During the early part of her menstrual period, a girl may want to cut down on strenuous games and play. But mostly she can lead her usual life. She may also feel a little tired and somewhat cranky. These feelings go away after a day or two.

In adolescence most girls become more interested in boys. They want to be with boys and learn to know them as friends. Girls are likely to whisper and giggle about boys. They begin to care a lot about how they look. They may take hours fixing their hair and choosing their clothes. They may start to use makeup.

Teen-age girls, like teen-age boys, may seem pretty silly to their younger brothers and sisters. But the girls are really learning about boys. They are learning how to get along with boys and how to attract them. It is helpful to know these things as they grow up.

Girls usually reach puberty a year or two before boys do. This shows in their earlier body changes, their earlier growing spurts, and their earlier interest in the other sex. For most girls, the ovaries do not begin to produce ripe eggs until some time after they reach puberty and begin to menstruate. A few girls, however, can become pregnant even before they first menstruate. There is no single pattern of growth.

After puberty both boys and girls feel more pleasure from handling their genitals. A young person may handle or rub his or her own genitals on purpose to have pleasure. This is called *masturbation*. Masturbation for these young people is a very common part of growing up and discovering their own bodies and the feelings their bodies can give them.

Masturbation is harmless to the body. Yet many boys and girls are told that it is bad, or that it is bad for them. Many adults have been taught and believe that it is harmful. Some religions say that masturbation is a sin. If young people feel that masturbation is bad or sinful, they may try to avoid it, and thus avoid the guilty feeling. But we wish to emphasize that there is no harm from masturbating except the guilt it makes some people feel. (There is no harm from *not* masturbating either.) Each person will decide about masturbation for him or herself. Like all other sexual activity, it is a private matter.

Adolescence is not always an easy time for boys and girls. Their bodies are going through big changes. These changes do not all come at the same time. One part of the body can be ahead of another part. This can make a boy or girl awkward and clumsy for a while.

Other kinds of changes happen during adolescence, too—changes in feelings, in mood. These changes go along with the body changes. Boys and girls in adolescence often daydream. They sometimes fight against their families and schools. They may have times of feeling very sad and low. They worry about themselves. Change may be hard for them.

One thing that sometimes makes adolescence difficult is the way young people reach puberty at different ages (see Figure 22). One boy may start his body changes when he is eleven. Another may not begin until he is fifteen or sixteen. The second boy may worry when he is thirteen or fourteen because his body is still like a child's body, and his genitals are not as fully developed as the first boy's. One girl may start to

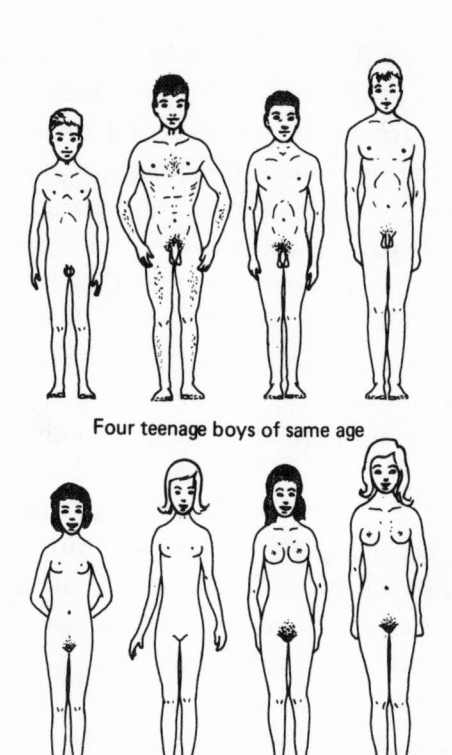

Four teenage boys of same age

Four teenage girls of same age

Figure 22

menstruate when she is ten, another not until she is sixteen. The second may worry when she is thirteen or fourteen because her body, and especially her breasts, are not as fully developed as the first girl's.

All these boys and girls are normal. The truth is that people just develop differently. Even so, friends who reach puberty at different rates may not understand each other. One wants to date, the other hates the idea, and so on. Somebody is likely to feel hurt or

57

left out. They will all catch up by their late teens, but there will be some hard times for some of them first. It is a little easier if they understand what is going on and know that it is going to happen that way.

By the end of adolescence, young people do not depend on their parents the way they did when they were children. This does not mean that they have no more to do with their parents. But it gives them the chance to know and love their parents in a different way—as friends and advisers, perhaps, and eventually, in most cases, as the grandparents of their own children.

Becoming a grown-up. The last step in a person's growing is becoming a grown-up, or adult. Adults, unless they are handicapped in some way, are able to take care of themselves, to go to work, to have families of their own, and to support them.

In our society this step comes anywhere between eighteen and twenty-five or even later. It depends on the person and the kind of life he or she expects to lead. More and more people are going on to college and graduate school after high school, and this delays the time when they go to work. These people generally depend on their families longer than young people who start jobs right after high school.

Adults' bodies have stopped growing. Girls reach this point in their late teens, boys in their early twenties. They will be no taller or broader-boned, though they may gain some weight. (One small child said, "A grown-up is a person who has stopped growing on both

58

ends and started growing in the middle.") Grown-ups'
energy can turn from growth to work.[Q11, 12]

This adulthood is what all the growth has been for.
New adults begin on the most satisfying and useful part
of their lives. They know their own bodies now. They
are used to them. They have caught up with themselves. Now they can give themselves more readily to
people and jobs outside themselves.

CHAPTER 10

HOW WE LEARN TO BE
MEN AND WOMEN

During all their lives people have body pleasures. They
have pleasure from smelling, tasting, seeing, and listen-
ing and from the feelings different parts of their bodies
give them. Grown people also have pleasure in being
men or being women. These feelings make up people's
sexuality.

Sexuality gives pleasure. It is an exciting part of
being grown up. You are now growing toward full sexuality at your own speed. You know some people who
grow in height fast and others who grow just a little
each year. The same is true of sexuality. Each of you
has your own timetable—right for you—for growing
into manhood or womanhood. Some grow quickly,
some gradually. And each stage of growth is important,
with its own kinds of fun and pleasure and learning.

Adult men and adult women are alike in many ways. They are both people—*human beings*. They both have all the strengths and weaknesses of human beings. Both may tell the truth, or both may lie. Both are able to share and to be honest. They may also be selfish and dishonest. Both men and women have pleasure and pain. Both can very much enjoy the sex act.

But men and women are different in many ways, too. They are different in their bodies and tend to be different in some of their feelings; for example, in their sex feelings. A man may feel sex quickly and strongly in his penis, although other parts of his body feel sexual, too. A woman is likely to feel sex more slowly and with her whole body—though her feeling may also be very strong, especially in her clitoris and the area around it.

People start learning to be men or women just as soon as they are born. Right away they tend to be treated as boys or as girls, not just as babies. People *teach* boys and girls how they are supposed to act, both by what they *say* and by what they *do*. Children copy what older people do. From all the teaching and copying, boys and girls gradually *learn* how to be men and women.

For children growing up, it is important how people around them see men and women. If people think men are always supposed to be strong, work outside the house, and avoid housework, then boys and girls will think that way, too. If people think girls are weak and soft and should grow up only to be wives and housekeepers, boys and girls will think that way, too. This

60

can make it hard for young people to develop all their interests and talents. In our society now, it is more and more common for men to do and enjoy things that used to be only for women, and women are able to do and enjoy things that used to be "for men only." A man can be gentle and tender, for example. It isn't just women who are that way. Men, too, can cry when someone is hurt. They can comfort small children. They can write poetry, paint pictures, be ballet dancers —and still be men.

A woman can be strong and capable. It isn't just men who are that way. A woman can earn the family living. Women can do repairs or mow the lawn. They can be doctors, design bridges, run races—and still be women.

CHAPTER 11

MARRIAGE

When boys and girls grow up, they are ready to live away from their families. Sooner or later they generally choose marriage as the way they will live and express their sexual feelings.

We can say that a man and a woman are married when they decide to live together and form a family. They may have a big wedding or a small one. They may be married in a church or at home or in a judge's office. They may sometimes just start living together.

No matter how they decide to be married, their marriage tells other people that they expect to live together permanently and probably have children.

There are many reasons why couples choose to be married, even though it is possible for them to have intercourse and children without marrying. For one thing, it is against the laws and customs in most places for them to live together without being married. For another, they probably want their joining together to be permanent.

The man and woman generally want to set up a family and a home that will give each of them and their children love and support and a place where they belong. They probably marry because they love each other. Marriage gives the couple and the family a strong foundation. It gives all human society strength, because it means that people can count on the relationship's continuing.

It is important to remember that most married men and women are ordinary people. This means that they are not perfect. Their marriage may sometimes not seem to be perfect, either. No matter how much a man and woman enjoy each other and love each other, there are times when they disagree. They may have arguments, shout at each other, and even occasionally hit each other. None of these things has to mean that a marriage is bad or that the man and woman wish they were not married.

Most people, married or unmarried, have to let off steam sometimes. Married people often do it by arguing with each other. In most marriages that last, the man and woman agree more than they disagree. They work together more than they fight. They respect each other more than they blame each other for their troubles.

Divorce. Some marriages do not last as long as the man and woman live. A couple may marry and later decide that their marriage is not good. They may decide to separate. This means the man and woman do not live together any more. If they want to be able to marry again, they must be *divorced.* They must go to a court and show a judge why they want to end their marriage. If the judge gives them a divorce, he or she makes a decision that they are not married any longer. Then the law says they may marry again.

Some religions do not allow divorce. This means that people of those religions are not supposed to marry again as long as their first mate is alive, even if a judge has given them a divorce.

There can be many reason for divorce. The couple may have married too quickly. They may have no children. Sometimes the man or the woman wants to marry another person. Mental illness, cruelty, one partner leaving the other—all these can be reasons for divorce.

Divorce is likely to be hard for the man and woman. It is likely to be hard for their children, too, if they have children. It means dividing up family members and property in ways that are often difficult. But, for all in the family, divorce is often better than going on with an unhappy marriage. Children sometimes suffer because they think they are to blame for their parents' divorce, but that is most unlikely to be true.

Widows and Widowers. Another group of people who are no longer married are those whose mates have died. A woman whose husband is dead is called a *widow.* A man whose wife is dead is called a *widower.* Most widows and widowers are older people, in their sixties, seventies, or eighties. But there are young widows and widowers, too, whose husbands or wives died at a fairly early age. Some widows and widowers marry again; some do not.

People Who Have Not Married. Marriage is not necessary or right for every grown-up. There are some people who never marry. Some of them do not want to take care of a family. Some find it hard to live so closely with another person. Some are homosexual, or gay, sexually attracted to their own rather than the opposite sex.[Q13] Sometimes people lose the one person they wanted to spend their lives with, and so they never marry.

Some people do not marry because they decide to give all their energy and lives to a religion, or to a job, or to something else they believe in very much. For example, priests and nuns in the Roman Catholic Church are not supposed to marry. In certain parts of the world, people may decide to spend their lives praying and thinking, and they do not marry.

Perhaps you know some grown-ups in their twenties or thirties who are not married. If you talk with them you may find that they want to be married some day.

64

These people are willing, perhaps happy, to put off the pleasures of marriage for a few years. They have time to know many people of the opposite sex. When they do marry, they may be happier, because they have taken the time to find out what kind of marriage they want.

It is not always easy for young adults to choose the age when they will marry. Sometimes their families push them to pick a mate before they are ready. It may be the custom for people to marry at a certain age. If it is, people who wait may seem strange, and they may have a hard time. But those who marry only when they are sure they want to marry, and when they are sure they have found the right mate, are likely to find marriage most satisfying.

CHAPTER 12

MATING DOES NOT ALWAYS MAKE BABIES

To have babies is not the only reason why men and women mate. There are many other important reasons. Suppose a man and a woman are very much in love. This can mean many things. It can mean that they like and respect each other. It can mean that they want to make life good for each other, to feel responsible for each other always. Being in love can mean the man and woman want to feel very close to each other, to share their lives and thoughts and feelings and bodies very deeply with each other.

For this man and woman, having sexual intercourse can be one of the best and most enjoyable ways of expressing and strengthening their feeling for each other. Sex gives them great pleasure together. They have a strong, warm feeling for each other. This feeling spreads to things outside themselves, too. It makes them feel better about their family, their friends, their work, their whole lives.

The man and woman often may want to have intercourse and still be sure that no baby will come. This could be because they are not yet ready to take care of a family, because they already have as many children as they can take care of, or because they want to let one baby grow to a certain age before they have another. Or both the mother and the father may be working, and neither wants to be kept home by having a baby to care for.

There is another reason for limiting the number of children a couple has—a world reason. In the old days, a man and wife had to have a lot of children to be sure that some would grow up and start families of their own. Now, with good health care, most children do grow up and form families. If each of these children has a large family, and if each child in that family grows up and marries and has a large family, there will be many more people on the earth. They soon will be so crowded together that life will be very different for all of them, probably much more difficult, perhaps disastrously so. For example, there will be more people than the world can grow food for, unless food production and distribution are very carefully planned for the whole world. Now, with almost 4 billion people on earth, people are crowded and starving in many places. By the year 2000, there will probably be 6 or 7 billion people.

One way to avoid this rapid population growth is for couples to plan for smaller families. To help with *family planning*, doctors have found methods that couples can use so that they can have intercourse and usually not have babies. These are methods of *contraception* (sometimes called *birth control*). They are ways of keeping the sperm and egg from joining together.[Q14]

Most couples who want children can have them. But there are some who are not able to have children, perhaps because their reproductive organs have been damaged by disease or did not develop as they should. A couple who want children even though they cannot have any of their own may *adopt* children. They may take into their family children whose natural parents cannot take care of them. Adopted children belong to the new parents. They are loved just as other children are loved by their parents.

CHAPTER 13

SOME PROBLEMS CONNECTED WITH SEX

Sex is one of the strongest forces in human life. Some people have made it the most important thing in their lives. But there are many ways to use human energy. Sex is one. Hard physical work is one. Thinking is one. Playing music, reading, writing, playing games or sports are other ways. Making friends and enjoying and entertaining them are still others. Traveling, studying, working, caring for a family are all ways of using energy. Too much attention to sex can mean a person misses out on these other parts of living and leads an unbalanced, unsatisfying life in the long run.

Some other people have worried so much about the strength of sex that they have pretended that it does not exist. Fifty or a hundred years ago, "nice" people would not admit that they ever thought about sex. Women especially were not told by their parents or teachers about this strong force in themselves. A book like this one could not have been written and published.

Even today, many of us have somehow learned to hide our thoughts about sex. You probably know adults who find it very hard to talk freely about sex. You may find it hard yourself.

But trying to believe that sex does not exist makes a problem. Sex does exist for all of us. If we try to bury it, we miss one of the great pleasures and strengths we might enjoy. Sex is a thing we need to talk about, a thing we need to know about, a thing we need to recognize as part of ourselves.

There is another kind of problem connected with sex. A few grown people become confused about sex in their lives. Instead of being attracted to adults of the opposite sex, they may be sexually attracted to children and try to have sex with them. This may be because they are sick or very unhappy. They may be that way all their lives, but more often they are confused about sex only when things are going wrong for them in other ways.

When you know that people sometimes misuse sex, you are better able to deal with them if they approach you. If strangers offer you candy to get you to come with them, if they ask you to go for a ride in a car, or if they seem to want to touch and pester you, you have to say "no" to them and walk quickly away. If some older person you know tries to touch you more than you like, especially if he or she tries to touch your genitals, you should not let him or her be alone with you. You should realize that he or she may be sexually interested in you. You should immediately tell your parents or someone else you trust. Perhaps the person can

69

be helped to change his or her sex interests. In any case you should stay away from him or her, whether you are a boy or a girl.

CHAPTER 14

MANY KINDS OF LOVE

People can love each other in many different ways. Over the years that people know each other their love can grow. Generally, love begins with *self-love*. This may seem strange to you. You may think of people who love themselves a lot as being selfish. But really selfish people are probably *not* sure of themselves. They are not sure they are as good as they ought to be. Therefore, they cannot give themselves easily to other people. They do not really love and respect themselves enough.

But think about people who *are* sure of themselves. They know their own value. They are not worried about whether they are good enough. These are the sorts of people who can love other people, too. They respect the one person they know best—themselves— and they can give the same respect to others.

Children learn *self-respect* or self-love from their families and those close to them. If they love you and respect you, you learn that you are a valuable person. You love yourself and you can love others in turn.

70

Another kind of love is *parental love*—that is, love of parents for their children. Probably you have enjoyed this kind of love. Even when your parents punish you or think what you do is wrong, you know that they keep on loving you as a person.

Beside self-respect and parental love, there is the kind of love you may feel with a very close friend. We might call it *close friendship*. You are happy when you are together. You can talk about anything and everything. Each of you has a fuller life because of the other person.

Another kind of love grows up between people who are doing a job together that they enjoy and believe in. People who share a hobby like stamp collecting or an interest like music may get together over shared projects and feel a sort of love for each other. We can call this kind of love *comradeship*.

A person who recognizes the special value of every one of the other people in the world and who loves all people has *brotherly love*. Such a person is likely to want to help others, both nearby and far away.

There is another, powerful kind of love, the kind of love we have been writing about especially in this book. A man and a woman—or sometimes two men or two women—may be drawn together by a strong *sexual* attraction, an attraction to each other's body.

The love that leads to marriage may combine all of the kinds of love we have talked about: self-respect, parental or supporting love, close friendship, comradeship, brotherly love, and sexual love. Or a marriage

71

may start off with only one or two of these kinds of love. After marriage, as the couple live together, and if they are considerate of each other, their love will probably grow and become more complete, satisfying their needs for both sexual love and many of the other kinds, too.

PART II

FAMILIES: SOME HISTORY AND SOME DIFFERENCES

CHAPTER 15

HOW MAN BEGAN TO LIVE
IN FAMILIES

Perhaps you have studied about dinosaurs. If so, you
know that when dinosaurs lived on the earth there
were no people. Man had not developed yet. Then
the dinosaurs died. The last ones lived perhaps 100
million years ago. Men have been on the earth for
only about 2 million years (see Figure 23).

Men did not suddenly appear. They developed
slowly from other animals. In the time of the dinosaurs, there were some small, sharp-toothed creatures
that lived by gnawing with their teeth. Some of these,
over millions of years, gradually developed into animals much like the apes and monkeys that are living
now. These ancient animals probably lived in forests.
They ate leaves and berries and fruit. They ran on
all fours, and they had feet and hands that could
hold on to branches for climbing (see Figure 24). Both
men and present-day monkeys and apes probably come
from these animals.

An animal that is just right for the kind of life he
leads does not need to change. Change comes when an

75

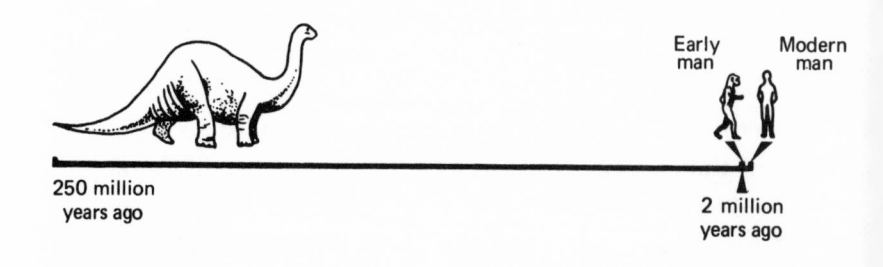

Early man

Modern man

250 million years ago

2 million years ago

Figure 23

animal is not right for what he finds around him. Then his group has to change, or it cannot go on living. That is what happened to the dinosaurs. They were just right for living in swamps and eating swamp-growing plants. Then, during a period of 10 to 20 million years, the swamps dried up and the plants changed. The dinosaurs did not change enough to live outside of swamps. Gradually they all died.

But the small, sharp-toothed creatures were better at changing. If you remember what you read in Chapter 6, you can figure out how the changes came about. Remember, different children receive different characteristics from their parents. This is true of animals as well as people. The young that receive the most useful

76

characteristics are likely to be the ones who live long enough to reproduce. They pass their useful characteristics on to their own young. As this process goes on for many generations, the animals can change quite a lot from their *ancestors*—the animals that came before them.

The ancestors of today's monkeys and apes probably went on living in forests, and they did not need to change much to go on living. But the ancestors of

What the common ancestor of man
and apes may have looked like

Figure 24

human beings started to live on the ground, on plains where there were not many trees. (This may be because the weather grew dry and the trees on many parts of the earth gradually died out.) People needed to change in many ways in order to survive.

There were two main changes in our ancestors: (1) they began to stand upright; and (2) they began to eat

77

a lot of meat. Standing upright leaves people's hands free to carry things. They can make and use tools. Standing upright also means it is easier for them to look all around and see things that are far away (see Figure 25).

When the ancestors of people started to live away from the forest, they had to find new things to eat. They ate other animals—that is, meat. To get meat they began to *hunt* animals for food. Early people had

Figure 25

to hunt to live. From their hunting life grew many of their ways of living, ways we still follow today.

There are plenty of leaves and berries and fruits in the forest and it is quite simple to get them. Therefore, the apes that live in the forest do not need to work together to get food for the group. They travel around

78

together, but each one gets his or her own food (except that mothers help their babies).

But as hunters, people had a problem. They could not run as fast as many animals. One person chasing one animal would not be likely to catch it. The women were sometimes not able to hunt at all. When they were pregnant or nursing a baby, or taking care of little children, they could not leave home for many hours or even days to hunt for food.

Therefore, early people had to work together—to *cooperate*—to find food. They cooperated in groups. The men left home to hunt together. Several men could outsmart one animal even if the animal could run faster than the men could. The women stayed home, took care of the children, and waited for the men to bring in the meat.

People learned to plan ahead, to know when they were going to need food and hunt for it. They learned to *communicate,* to tell each other what they knew and what they planned to do. That was the beginning of language.

Gradually the idea of permanent couples must have grown among early men and women. With permanent couples, each man would have a woman and children to come back to after the hunt. Each woman and her children would have a man to bring them food and protect them. Families and lasting love between men and women probably developed as a result of the hunting way of life.

Men, not women, undoubtedly were the heads of their families even in earliest times. Men usually are stronger and bigger than women. Hunting increased the man's strength. And the whole family counted on the man for food to keep them alive. The man also knew more about the world because he saw more of it than did the home-bound woman. So the father was the strongest member of the family, he knew the most about the outside world, and he was the boss. Of course today, with modern conveniences and ways of sharing work and responsibility, these differences between men and women are much less important.

Early people's way of living meant that intelligence —brain power—was very valuable. Brain power enabled people to think ahead, to plan a hunt, to arrange family life. With their brains they could figure out ways to make tools and use them. They could get other people to understand and learn what they were doing. The person who was good at these things was much better off than the one who could not do them well. So intelligence was a useful characteristic, and it developed very rapidly in human beings. (Don't forget, people have been developing their intelligence for 2 million years.)

When human beings became more intelligent, they collected more knowledge—they knew more. Then it took them longer to teach it all to their children. The children of human beings, therefore, had to be dependent on their parents longer than any other animals. They needed time to learn. Apes take between five and ten years to become adult. For human beings, it is ten to fifteen years before they are able to reproduce; boys are not fully grown until their twenties, girls not until their late teens. And human beings are the only animals who keep their curiosity—their wish to learn new things—even after they are fully grown.

For all these reasons, love and families and marriage grew as a bond between people. Families were a good way to work together and to raise children. They made a base for each person, a home for him or her to belong and come back to. Without a family way of living, human beings probably could not have survived in the world.

CHAPTER 16

TWO WAYS OF LIFE
DIFFERENT FROM OURS

Early people set up the pattern for human living: marriage and families, and group cooperation. Groups of people—relatives, neighborhoods, cities, countries—still cooperate and work together. Communication is even more important than it was. We have learned not only to talk, but to write and to send messages and pictures over long distances. And there is much more knowledge to remember and teach.

These things are true almost everywhere in the world. But people in some parts of the world have developed ways of living that are different from ours. We shall look at only two groups of people, the Iroquois Indians and the Japanese. We shall see how they built quite different ways of life. But both the Iroquois and the Japanese use the basic pattern for living set up by early people.

The Iroquois Indians. When the first people from Europe were settling in America, the Iroquois were one of the biggest and best organized groups of Indians. They lived in what is now the Northeastern United States, especially upper New York state. They controlled much of the eastern part of our country (see Figure 26).

With the Iroquois, men were the leaders. But women had a lot of power, too. The older women of

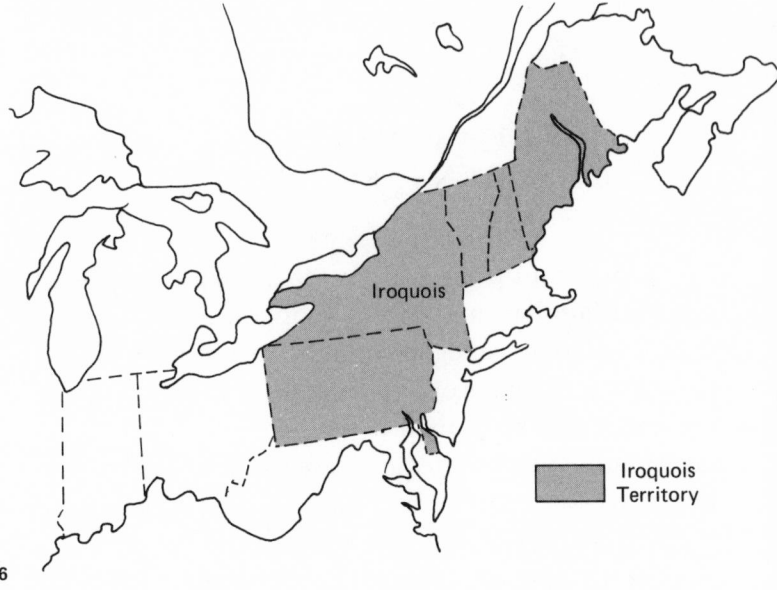

Iroquois
Territory

Figure 26

the village and the tribe had the right to name the chieftains. They named men. The men decided whether the group would go to war or live in peace and other important matters. Of course, the women could change the chiefs if they did not like what was going on. But the chiefs, men, made the big decisions while they were chiefs.

82

Iroquois Indians lived in *longhouses*. These were sometimes 80 to 100 feet long, made of birch bark over a wood frame. There was a central corridor from one end of the house to the other. There were walls that divided the house into sections, with one fireplace for each two sections. Four families shared a fireplace (see Figure 27).

The longhouses were owned by women. The oldest and strongest woman was in charge of the whole house. When a daughter of one of the women married and

Figure 27

had children, the new family lived in one of the rooms of the longhouse. The husband did not take his wife away; he joined her. The wife kept her own name, too. She did not use her husband's name as wives in the United States do now. Names, houses, and fields passed down from mother to daughter, not from father to son as is the case with us. (This system is called *matrilineal,* which means that it is the mother's side of the family that counts.)

The main jobs of Iroquois men were to hunt animals for food and to fight in wars. They also cleared the trees off fields to be used for planting, and they built fences around the villages. The women did almost everything else. They put up the houses, farmed the land, cooked, sewed, took care of children. They worked in groups. For instance, all the women from one village or longhouse planted and cultivated and harvested crops together. The older women helped the ones who were expecting babies or who had young children.

The children were very much loved by the adults. They were brought up freely. There were not many rules, and the children did not get into much trouble. Each child belonged to the whole longhouse family, not just to one father and mother. He called all the women near his mother's age "mother," all the children "brother" or "sister," and all the oldest women "grandmother." The children were gradually taught what they needed to know as men or women. When they were old enough they joined the hunting parties or the women's work.

Boys and girls did not choose whom they were going to marry. Children belonged to their mother, and a mother chose a husband for her daughter. The chosen boy came to live at the girl's longhouse—he always had to be from a different longhouse. The new husband helped with the men's work of the longhouse, but he never was really a member of that house. He stayed a member of his mother's house, even though he did not live there any more. Children of the marriage belonged to the wife's longhouse.

Though this system is different from ours in many ways, it seems to have worked well. The women and children were together in a group that could keep life going while the men were away. The men were good fathers, and also brave and strong hunters and fighters. They were so successful that the Iroquois became a very large and strong group of tribes. Both the women and the men were respected, useful, and apparently happy in what they had to do.

The Japanese. Japan is a powerful modern nation and also a very old one. Many Japanese people today still live according to patterns which have changed very little over many, many years.

In Japan, traditionally the oldest man in a family receives the most respect. He manages all the family's affairs. The other men in the family have a rank according to their age—the second oldest is the second most important, then the third oldest, and so on. Then come the women, ranked by age, too.

Any man is more important than any woman. Then

it is age that counts the most. Each person has to respect and obey anyone who is older or has a higher rank. Such a system is called a *hierarchy*.

In Japan there is a hierarchy in the family and in the nation, too. For Japanese adults there are many rules about how to act, who is in charge, and what to do about insults or slights from other people. Much of life is governed by rules.

Children must prepare for all the rules of grown-up life. So, you might think that parents would not allow boys and girls much freedom. You might think that children would have rules piled on them, too, so that they will know how to behave when they grow up. It does not work that way. Japanese children are very free. They can play games and shout things that would get adults into real trouble, and nothing happens to them. They are "spoiled" by grandparents, allowed to have tantrums, run freely in the streets even at three years old.

When they are taught, young children are not scolded if they go wrong. They are just *expected* to do the right thing—and they generally do it. Small children are taught how to sit still and how to do certain jobs. An adult teaches them by putting their bodies in the proper position or moving their hands in the right way. They are not *told* what to do; their bodies are *made* to do it by someone who knows how. They keep being made to do it until they have learned the way from habit.

When the children grow older they begin to go to school. Now they gradually learn the rules that tell them how to behave in the adults' world. They learn to worry about what other people will think of them. They worry very much about being laughed at and made to look foolish. They learn their own "place" and the "place" of each other person. Their life goes from freedom and ease to strict rules and difficult patterns. When they reach sixty years of age, some of the rules will be let up. In the meantime all their days are organized according to their place and their duty.

Marriage is generally planned for young men and women by their parents. The young people do not choose mates for themselves. When an oldest son marries, he brings his wife to live in his parents' house. His father is in charge of the family until he dies, and then the son takes over. The son's mother manages the household, and the son's wife has nothing to say about it. She must do what her mother-in-law says. Women do the work of the household, and they are expected to serve the men on their knees. Men work outside the house, at business, the professions, farming.

The Japanese way has produced a very successful and powerful country, even if we think it may be hard on the women. The Iroquois were more able to find a way to make life good for both sexes.

Think of the difference between the Japanese way of life and life in our country. Here, the smaller the children, the more rules there are about what they may and may not do. As they grow older, they are allowed to do more and more things. There are fewer and fewer rules. Adults have the greatest freedom of all. They can do what they want with their lives. Women are quite important and do not have to bow to the men in everything. This is opposite to what happens in Japan. Yet both systems work. Both systems have produced strong and rich countries, highly able and highly trained people, and beautiful works of art.

The Japanese and the Iroquois are just two of the peoples who have worked out successful patterns of life. There are many, many others, all different in some ways. You may be interested to read about some of the others—about the Indians of India, the Eskimos of North America, the Lapps of northern Europe, the Masai or the Bushmen of Africa, for example.

Human beings set up different patterns of living to suit their own special ideas of what is right and valuable and good. All the patterns are built in some degree on the ways of early people—on marriage and families and group cooperation.

PART III

OTHER WAYS OF
REPRODUCING: ANIMALS
AND PLANTS

CHAPTER 17

HOW ANIMALS REPRODUCE:
FISH, FROGS, BUTTERFLIES,
AND BIRDS

In the early chapters of this book you read about how human babies are started, how they grow inside their mothers, how they are born, and how they grow up. All of this is called *human reproduction*. From this chapter and the next two you can learn about reproduction in animals and plants.

The way human beings reproduce themselves is very much like the way some animals do. But it is quite different from the way other animals reproduce. Nature has tried out many ways of reproduction in the animal world. It does not even always take both a male and a female to produce young.

Some very simple, one-celled creatures can reproduce all by themselves—for example, the *amoeba*. The single cell merely divides into two new separate cells, or into many new cells (see Figure 28). Other small animals reproduce by budding—for example, the *sponge*. Small bumps or buds form on the surface of the body. These break off and form complete new creatures (see Figure 29).

With these kinds of reproduction a single animal reproduces by itself. There is little chance for change or development of that particular kind of animal. Each creature produces exact copies of itself over and over again. There is no combination of genes from a father and a mother. The genes of the offspring are the same as those of the parent.

Some very simple animals and most of the more

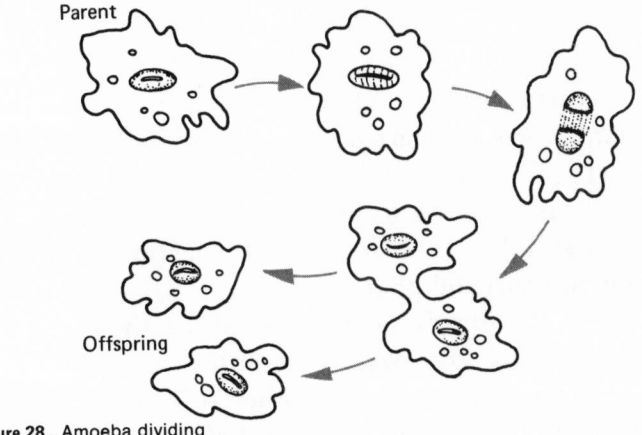

Figure 28. Amoeba dividing

complicated ones have other ways of reproducing. Their young combine genes from two parents, as human babies do. One-celled animals, such as those called *paramecia,* sometimes join together, exchange genes, and separate again. In more complicated animals, the female carries eggs which must be fertilized by the male's sperms to produce young. This is called *sexual reproduction.*

92

Fish. If you have ever eaten fish roe or caviar, you have eaten the eggs of a fish. The fish that the eggs came from must have been a female, of course. And the eggs were not fertilized when the fish was caught.

Large numbers of eggs ripen inside an adult female fish. When the eggs are ripe, the female is ready to lay them. A male fish is attracted to her. The female lays the eggs in the water (see Figure 30). The male then swims over the eggs and releases millions of sperms in a cloud of liquid called *milt*. The milt fertilizes the female's eggs. A very few fish, like the guppy, fertilize

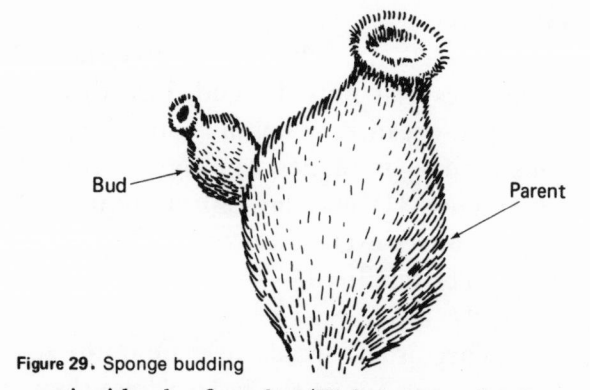

Bud → ← Parent

Figure 29. Sponge budding

the egg inside the female. (Fish have only one opening from their bodies for both reproduction and waste. This is the *cloaca*.)

Even though the eggs and the milt are released at almost the same time and in the same place, there is a good chance that many of the eggs will wash away and never be fertilized. Many of the fertile eggs die or are eaten before they become adult fish.

This kind of reproduction is not very efficient. There is no chance of getting one adult for each egg

93

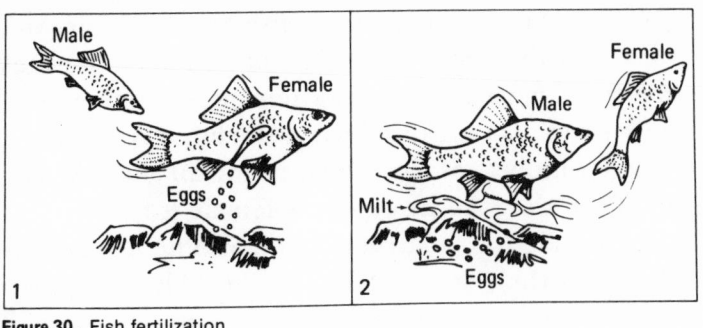

Figure 30. Fish fertilization

laid. A great many eggs must be laid by each female to make sure that some will develop into adult fish who can reproduce, too.

The more protection adult fish can give their eggs, the fewer the eggs that must be laid. Fish that reproduce in the open ocean may lay millions of eggs. Fish that protect their eggs in nests or by carrying them around (see Figure 31) may lay only hundreds. A female guppy produces even fewer eggs, since each one is more likely to be fertilized.

Frogs. Frogs are usually ready to mate in the spring, after they have come out of the holes where they have

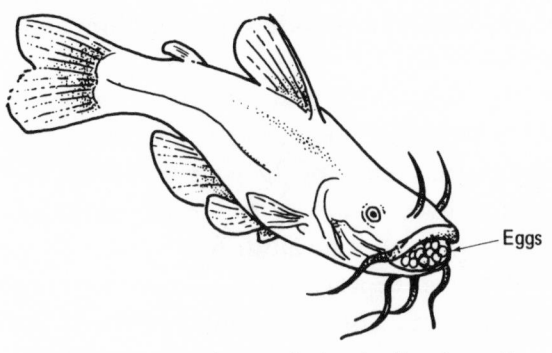

Figure 31. Fish protecting eggs by carrying them in mouth

94

spent the winter hibernating. They are likely to mate near water. The male frog climbs on the back of the female when she is ready to lay her eggs (see Figure 32). He fertilizes the eggs with his sperms as the eggs come from her cloaca. This means that there is quite a good chance that each egg will be fertilized.

A few kinds of frogs have ways of protecting their eggs after they have been laid. Some make nests for the eggs and guard them there. Others carry the eggs on their backs, on their legs, or in their mouths until they hatch.

When frog eggs hatch, tadpoles come out. Tadpoles

Figure 32. Frogs mating

look a lot like fish, with a head, body, and tail (see Figure 33). They have gills like fish. The tadpoles live in water. Gradually they begin to grow legs and to change to the shape of a frog. Finally, when they are no longer needed for swimming, their tails disappear.

Tadpoles live only in water, but most adult frogs live either on land or water. They are *amphibians*. Tadpoles cannot reproduce. Only when they become fully grown as frogs can they lay eggs that will hatch into tadpoles and eventually become frogs. Frogs lay many eggs that will never grow to reproduce themselves. The eggs or tadpoles may be eaten by fish or birds. Frogs themselves are eaten by birds, by snakes, and even by people. Each female frog lays a large number of eggs each mating season so that it is likely that some will grow to be adults. But a frog does not have to lay as many eggs as a fish does.

Butterflies. A caterpillar and a colorful butterfly do not look much alike. But the butterfly was once a caterpillar. And the caterpillar has all the body parts it needs to turn into a butterfly.

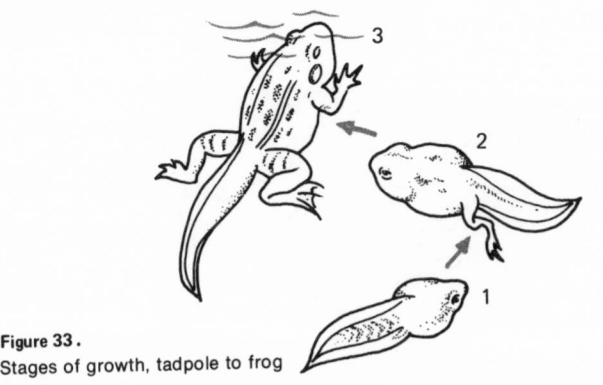

Figure 33.
Stages of growth, tadpole to frog

The young of butterflies go through four stages of growth (see Figure 34). First, *eggs* are laid by butterflies. From these eggs, *caterpillars* hatch. The caterpillars can move along the ground, but they cannot fly. They eat leaves and grow to their full size. Then they attach themselves to a branch or leaf and change into the third stage of growth.

In the third stage, a caterpillar becomes a *pupa* inside of a *chrysalis*. The pupa does not move or eat at

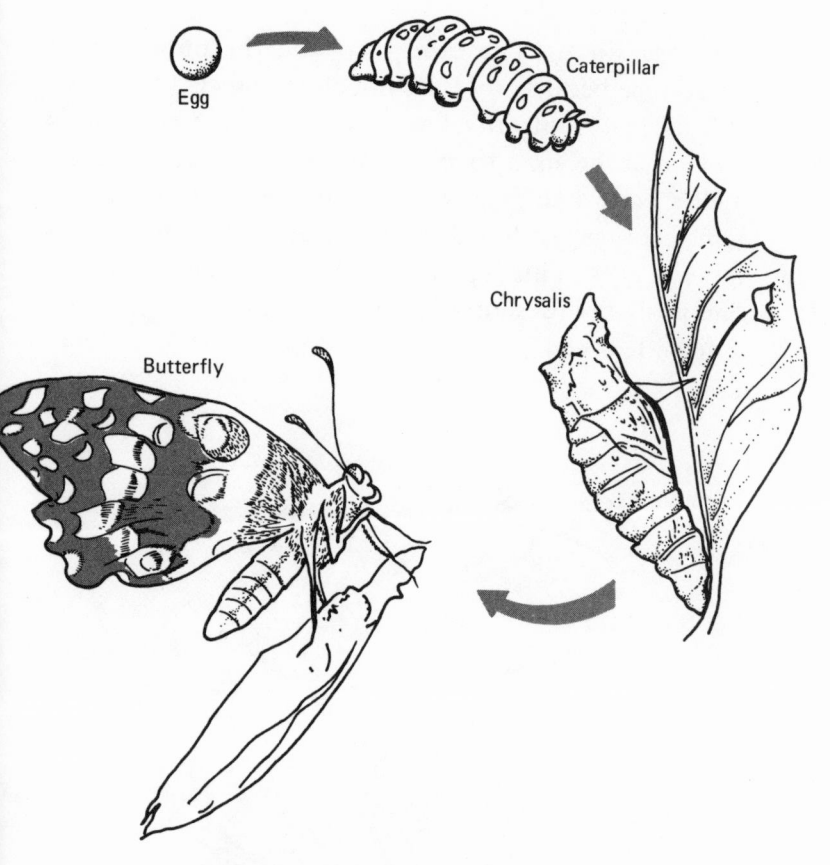

Figure 34. Stages of growth of a butterfly

all. It is becoming a butterfly. Its chrysalis generally matches the background so that it will not be too easily seen and the pupa eaten by birds or other enemies.

The fourth stage of growth is the *butterfly* itself. The butterfly comes out of the chrysalis when all the body-changes from caterpillar to butterfly have taken place. The butterfly does not grow—it often does not even eat. But it is the adult form of the insect. It can reproduce. (The caterpillar and the pupa cannot reproduce because they are not adult insects.)

The male butterfly has an organ at the end of his body that he uses to place his sperms inside the female's body (see Figure 35). The sperms fertilize the female's eggs, as they do in other animals. The female lays the eggs. This is generally the end of her life cycle. She probably dies after laying the eggs. The eggs start a new life cycle.

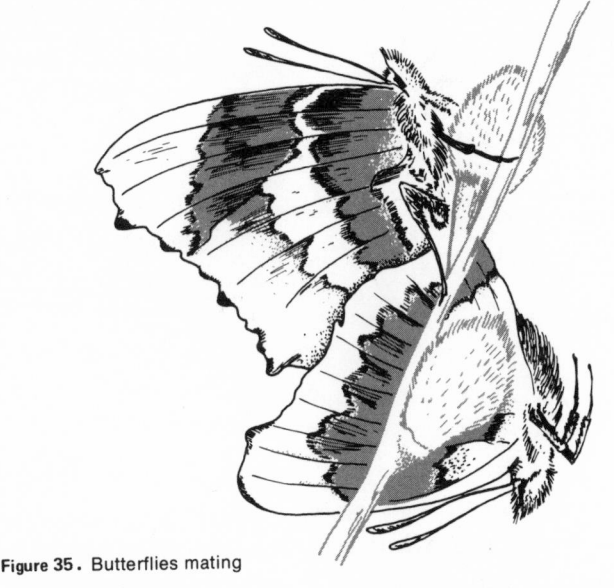

Figure 35. Butterflies mating

Birds. At the end of a long cold winter, in the city or the country, people are always glad to see their first robin. Then they are sure that spring is really coming. Some birds stay in the same place winter and summer. But others spend the winter in the warm south and then fly north to breed in the spring. They *migrate.*

98

When migrating birds arrive from the south, people know that spring is arriving, too.

Birds mate only when the female is producing ripe eggs from her ovaries. If these are produced in the spring, the fertilized eggs will hatch and the young will develop during the warm months of the year. They will have the greatest possible chance to find food, to keep warm, and to survive.

When they arrive at their breeding area, male birds will often choose a place for a nest. They will keep all other males away and try to get a female to come to the nesting place and breed with them. Male birds

Figure 36 . Male sage grouse ready to mate

have many different ways of attracting the females. They may be brightly colored like the cardinal or the pheasant. They may be able to puff themselves up to a large size like the sage grouse (see Figure 36). They may have special songs or make special noises, like the drumming of a partridge.

When birds finally do choose a mate, they are likely to keep the same mate for the whole breeding season. A few birds mate for life. Others mate only long enough to fertilize the eggs of the female.

Like fish, birds have a single opening from their

99

bodies—the cloaca—for both reproduction and waste. After their courtship, when they are ready for mating, the male bird climbs on his mate's back. He places his cloaca against hers and ejects his sperms. The female's eggs are fertilized inside her body and develop there for a time. Figure 37 shows the reproductive organs of a female bird and the path that the egg takes from the ovary until it is laid.

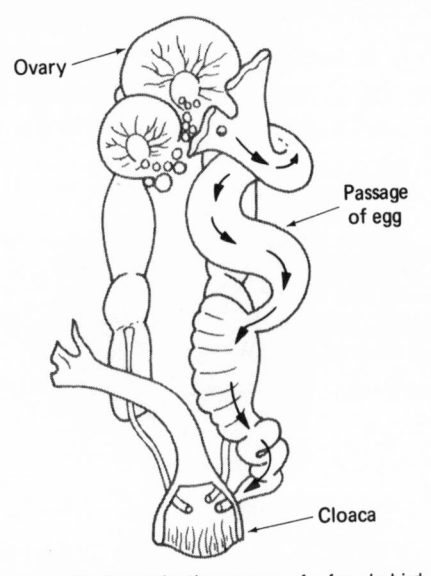

Figure 37. Reproductive organs of a female bird

The female bird lays her eggs in the nest that she and her mate have built. (Or one of the birds may have built it without help from the other.) She sits on the eggs to keep them warm until they hatch a few days to a few weeks later. Her mate may take turns with her, or he may bring her food while she is sitting on the eggs.

After the eggs hatch, the baby birds need care for

some time longer. They have to be fed and protected until they grow feathers and become strong enough to fly and feed themselves.

With all this help from their parents, young birds have a fairly good chance of growing to be adults themselves. But, still, most birds seem to need to lay several eggs at a time, sometimes more than once a season. Eggs may be lost or stolen or eaten, or the parent may not keep them warm enough to hatch. Young birds may be caught by snakes or cats or other animals before they are grown. They may not find enough to eat or they may be caught in a storm. Birds still must produce a good many eggs to be sure some will survive.

CHAPTER 18

HOW ANIMALS REPRODUCE: MAMMALS

Mammals are animals that feed their young with mother's milk. They are more or less covered with hair, and they generally produce living young rather than eggs. Mice, dogs, cows, bears, elephants are all mammals. Whales and porpoises are mammals; they are not fish, as you might think. Whales and porpoises bear live young and feed them with milk from the mother like other mammals. Human beings are mammals, too.

101

African elephant

Bear

Mouse

Dog

Man

Cow

Figure 38. Mammals (not drawn to scale)

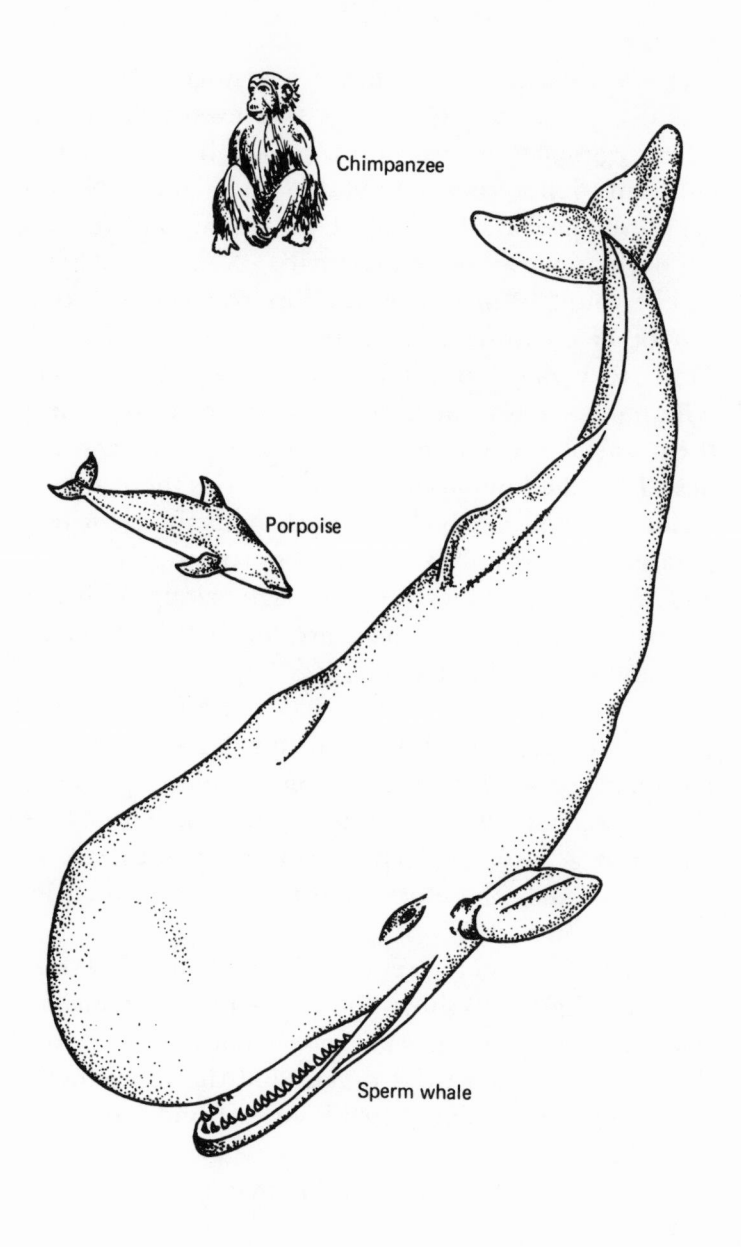

Chimpanzee

Porpoise

Sperm whale

As we have seen, most fish, frogs, insects, and birds produce young by laying eggs that eventually hatch. These eggs may receive a lot of care from their parents, but even so they are not safe from danger. Nature has developed a safer way of protecting and feeding the developing young in mammals.

The young of mammals develop from eggs the same way other creatures do, but the eggs are not laid. Instead, they develop inside the mother, not outside. The mother does ⸱ ot have to sit on her eggs to keep them warm. She does not have to protect her eggs in a nest. Like the human mother, she carries them around inside her, and her body keeps them at the right temperature. The mammal mother can run from enemies, and the young in her body go right along with her. Newly developing mammals are much safer than the eggs and young of other creatures.

These mammals, like man, have an efficient way of fertilizing eggs, too. All male mammals have a penis or a similar organ which they can use to place sperms inside the female's body. Sperms are not likely to be lost and an egg has a good chance of being fertilized. Female mammals therefore produce only one or a few eggs at a time.

Figure 39 shows the reproductive organs of a female dog, and Figure 40 shows the reproductive organs of a male dog. As you can see, there is not a great deal of difference between these organs and the reproductive organs of human beings (see Figures 1 and 5 on pages 22 and 28).

The ovaries of the female dog may produce several

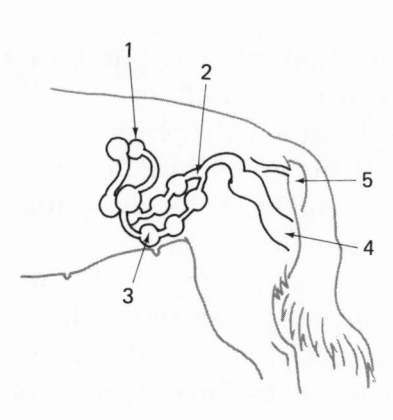

1. Ovary   2. Uterus
3. Lumps consisting of
   embryo and placenta
4. Vagina   5. Anus

Figure 39. Reproductive organs of a female dog

eggs at one time. If they are fertilized, these eggs develop in the uterus the way human eggs do. The embryos receive food from the mother through an umbilical cord and a placenta that is attached to the wall of the uterus. The puppies are born through the vagina. Each puppy is born still in the sac that held it in the uterus. The mother dog opens the sac with her teeth

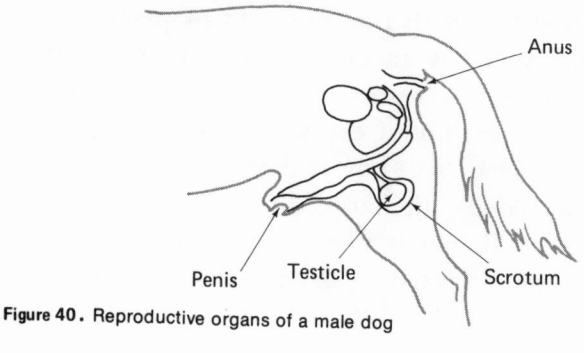

Figure 40. Reproductive organs of a male dog

and licks the puppy to start him breathing. She also bites off the umbilical cord for him. The mother dog usually eats the sac and the placenta—the afterbirth.

You can see from the figure that the female dog has two openings from her body, the vagina and the anus. She urinates from the vagina.

Mammals, except for man and some monkeys and apes, mate only at special times. They mate when the female is *in heat*. This is when her ovaries produce ripe eggs. The lining of her uterus thickens and grows richer, and her whole body prepares for the baby. When she is in heat, the female gives off special signs. She may produce smells or swellings or colorings that show the male that she is ready to mate.

When the male mammal smells or sees these special signs, he is excited sexually. He wants to mate with the female. We say the male is *in rut,* or rutting, at this time. Most mammals mate only when the female is in heat and the male is rutting, only when mating will produce offspring. (This is not so with human beings. There is no easy way to know when a human female produces a ripe egg. Human beings may mate at any time.)

Dogs are the animals that most of us know best, and we will use them as an example again, this time to show the mating habits of most mammals. A female dog comes in heat about every six months. Heat lasts for three weeks or so. The female's sex organs swell, and a little bloody discharge comes from her vagina. This has a smell that is very powerful for male dogs, and males are attracted to the female. In mating the male climbs on the back of the standing female, puts his erect penis in her vagina and deposits sperms there. You may have seen dogs doing this.

A female dog in heat may mate several times with the same dog, or with different dogs. She is most likely to start puppies—to conceive—after she has been in heat about ten days. When her period of heat is over, male dogs are no longer interested in mating with her. The male who has fathered puppies does not take on any duties as a father.

Puppies are born about two months after they are conceived. They need their mother's care for five or six weeks after that. Like human babies, newborn puppies get their food at first by sucking their mother's milk. A dog is full grown and ready to mate before he or she is one year old.

The time from the fertilization of the egg to the birth of the baby (this is called the *gestation period*) is different in different mammals. Generally, the bigger the animal, the longer the gestation period. The gestation period for a mouse is three weeks, for a dog two months, for a human being nine months, for a horse eleven months, and for an elephant twenty-one months.

But size is not the only thing that counts. Animals (like man) with more complicated brains have longer gestation periods than other animals the same size. And in some mammals, for example the fallow deer, the egg may not begin to develop as soon as it is fertilized. This makes the gestation period longer so that an egg fertilized in the fall will not develop into an animal ready to be born until spring.

When some mammals—horses and deer, for example—are born, they are able to walk and run and take care of themselves almost right away, although they still feed from their mother's milk. A foal (baby horse) takes only a few minutes to get on his feet after his birth. Other animals—puppies, for example—are almost helpless when they are born. They cannot stand, they cannot see, and they stay pretty much in one place. Animals that graze or browse (eat grass or shoots) and escape from danger by running produce young that can run right away. Animals that eat meat and escape danger by hiding produce young that stay helpless in nests hidden from enemies.

HOW PLANTS REPRODUCE

Plants, like animals, have different ways of reproducing, and the ways of plants are a lot like the ways of animals. Very simple, one-celled plants may reproduce by division, just as some simple animals do (see page 91).

More complicated plants have other ways of reproducing. Strawberry plants reproduce by sending out shoots or runners to start a new plant nearby. The branch of a vine bends down to the ground and puts down roots to start a new vine. Some trees work this way, too. Or a section of branch, cut from an existing plant, can be put in water or in the ground to root. Branches of plants can be made to grow on branches or roots of other plants. These are all ways of *vegetative* reproduction—no seeds are required.

The most highly developed plants have flowers and reproduce sexually. The flowers have both male and female cells as parts of them. When male and female cells grow together, seeds are produced. New plants grow from the seeds.

Figure 41 shows the main parts of a tulip flower. The *stamens* and the *pistils* are the parts used in reproduction. The stamen is the male part. It produces and stores a fine powder containing male reproductive cells. The powder is called *pollen*. The stamens of one flower may hold millions of grains of pollen.

The pistil is the female part of the flower. At its base is the flower's ovary. The egg cells of the plant grow inside the ovary. To start growing into a seed, the egg cell needs pollen. When a grain of pollen from a stamen sticks to the top of the pistil, the grain grows a pollen tube down inside the pistil to the ovary. The pollen tube joins with the egg cell, fertilizes it, and a seed starts to form.

The process of bringing the pollen to the pistil is called *pollination*. There are many ways of pollinating flowers. Some plants transfer pollen from their own stamens to their own pistils. Others are fertilized by pollen from other plants. The pollen may be carried from one plant to another by the wind. Or insects and birds, as they move from one flower to another, may carry the pollen.

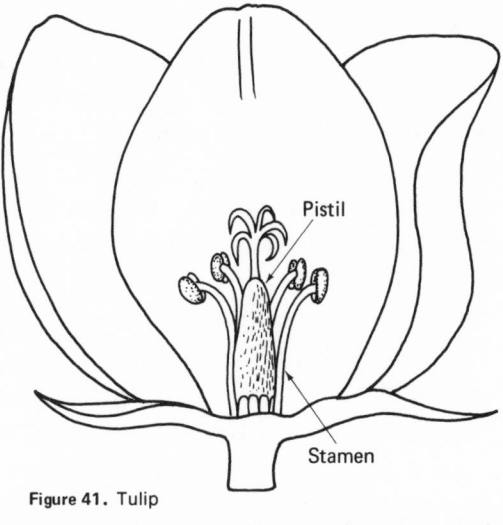

Figure 41. Tulip

For example, bees pollinate flowers. When they drink the nectar from a flower, pollen from the stamens rubs off on them (see Figure 42). The pollen fills pollen baskets on their legs. When the bees go to another flower, some of the pollen is likely to rub off on the pistil and pollinate that flower.

Flowers that pollinate themselves or are pollinated by the wind are usually not very bright or colorful. But flowers that depend on insects or birds for pollination are generally bright and showy. Such flowers are easy for the insects and birds to see, so they are likely to find them for food. They pollinate the flowers as they feed from them.

Once flowers have been pollinated and their seeds grow, the seeds have many ways of traveling to new places to grow into new plants. Birds or animals or people may eat the fruit around the seeds. The seeds pass

110

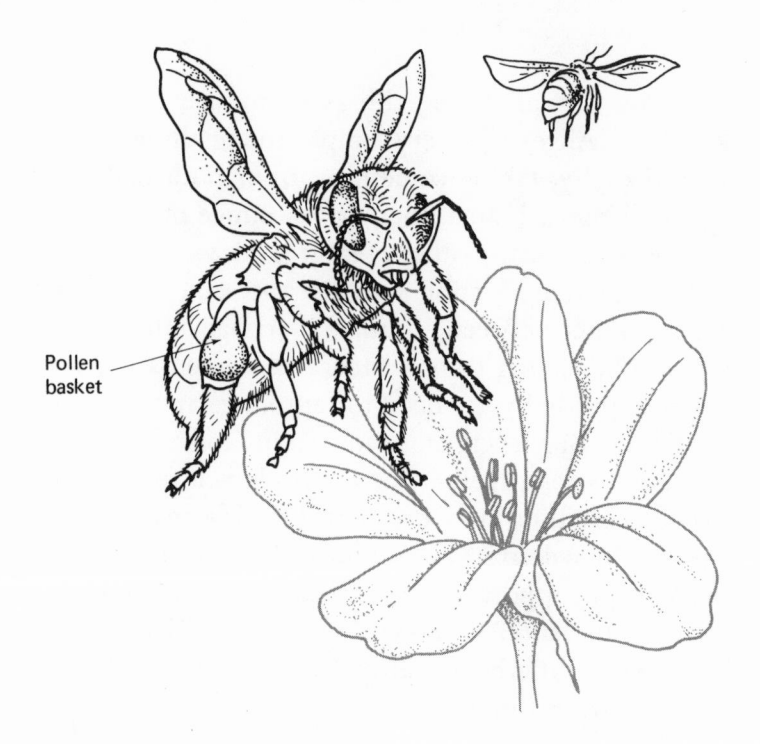

Pollen
basket

Figure 42 . Bee gathering pollen

through their bodies or are thrown away and drop in new places. Other kinds of seeds have wings or down or fluffy hairs that catch the wind. Still others have hooks or barbs or burrs that catch in the fur of animals. The animals carry the seeds to new ground. Other seed pods burst or explode so that their seeds are spread over a large area. Some seeds float on water to new places.

Many, many seeds are not fertilized or do not end up in good places to grow. Each plant produces a large number of seeds, sometimes as many as a million, so that some have a chance to survive.

So you see: all living things reproduce themselves somehow. All except very simple living things reproduce sexually, taking something from both male and female parents. Human beings reproduce in much the same way that many other creatures do.

Though reproduction is much the same, there is a big difference between a human marriage and the joining of other living things. Men and women are drawn together partly by the need to reproduce and continue their race. But, even more important today, they also develop a strong feeling for each other, a feeling that affects everything they do. It is a feeling that goes far beyond their desire to reproduce. We can call the feeling love, or support for each other, or respect, or enjoyment, or pleasure. Whatever we call it, it gives human life a very different quality from the lives of most other growing things.

QUESTIONS AND ANSWERS

When you read this book, you may have some questions about what it says. Or you may want to know more about certain things it talks about. We hope you will be able to ask your parents, your teachers, or some other adult about the things that interest you. In this section we have listed a few of the questions that may come up, and we have given answers for them.

Question 1: Why are a man's testicles on the outside of the body (in the scrotum) instead of inside the abdomen the way a woman's ovaries are?

Answer: Sperms live best in a temperature that is a little lower than the normal human body temperature of 98.6° F. In the scrotum the testicles can be a little cooler than they would be inside the man's body. In fact, when it is very hot, the scrotum hangs further from the man's body, and when it is very cold, the scrotum shrinks closer to his body, to keep the testicles at the best temperature for the sperms. If a man wears clothes so tight that his testicles are hotter than they should be, or if a man has a severe high fever, he may not be able to reproduce for a time. This is because sperms will not stay alive while the temperature in the testicles is too high.

Question 2: How many sperms does a man discharge when he has an ejaculation of semen?
Answer: The teaspoonful of semen that a man ejaculates usually has about 400 million sperms in it. Out of all these sperms, only one will fertilize the egg. When one sperm joins the egg, a sort of covering forms immediately around the egg. This stops other sperms from entering. But the other sperms are apparently needed. They probably help break down the wall of the egg so that one sperm can pass through it in the first place. A great many of the sperms do not reach the woman's tube in any case. Perhaps only four or five thousand swim that far.

Question 3: If the ovaries produce only one ripe egg every four weeks, how can two eggs be fertilized at the same time to produce fraternal twins?
Answer: If the ovaries always produced just one egg a month, then there could not be any fraternal twins. But every now and then the ovaries do not work on the usual timetable. Perhaps an egg ripens in each ovary at the same time, or two eggs ripen in one ovary. Then it is possible for two eggs to be fertilized at about the same time and for fraternal twins to be started.

Question 4: What are Siamese twins?
Answer: Siamese twins are identical twins born joined

114

together at some part of their bodies. This happens when a fertilized egg divides into two cells that separate almost all the way, but not quite. Both cells develop into babies, but the babies are joined to each other. Siamese twins can sometimes be separated by doctors, but this may not work if they share too many important parts of the body.

Question 5: Are half the babies that are born in the world boys and half girls?
Answer: No. More boys than girls are born all over the world. For each 100 girls that are born, there may be 105 or 106 boys. Even more boys are born in times of war or great hunger. Scientists are not sure why it happens, but sperms for boys are a little more likely to be the ones that fertilize the woman's eggs.

Question 6: How much bigger does a boy's penis grow during adolescence?
Answer: A boy's penis just about doubles in size during this time, to an average length of three to four inches (see page 29). His penis may be average in size, or it may be smaller or larger than average, just as he may be average in height, short, or tall. The size of his penis makes no difference in a man's ability to enjoy or give pleasure in sex. In fact, penises differ far less in size when they are erect than when they are limp.

Question 7: Can a boy have an erection before he reaches puberty?
Answer: Yes. Boys, and even babies, have erections. These generally happen when the boy has a full blad-

der and needs to urinate, or when clothing or bedding has been rubbing against his penis, or when he has been handling his penis. When the stimulation stops these erections end and the penis goes back to its normal size and position.

Question 8: When a boy has reached puberty, does having an erection always mean he will soon ejaculate sperm?
Answer: No. Most erections end without ejaculation.

Question 9: It says in Chapter 2 that a man's testicles are always making more sperms. What happens to the sperms if the man does not have intercourse?
Answer: After puberty, a boy or man who has no other sexual outlet may have *emissions* of semen, generally at night while he is sleeping (see page 52). They may happen frequently for some men and only once in a great while for others. Or more often the boy or man may release sperms in ejaculations brought on by masturbation, that is by handling his penis (see page 55).

Question 10: If a girl has a hymen that makes it hard for her to use tampons during menstruation, what happens when she is married and wants to have sexual intercourse?
Answer: As a girl grows older, the opening in her hymen may gradually grow larger. Or her first intercourse may stretch or break the hymen so that the opening is larger. In this case, the first intercourse may be a little painful and the hymen may bleed a little.

Sometimes the girl's doctor may decide that it is a good idea to make the opening in her hymen larger by a simple surgical operation, or she may gradually stretch the opening herself, using her fingers.

Question 11: Do people ever stop being able to have babies?
Answer: At about forty-five to fifty, women lose their ability to have children. This happens at *menopause,* when the ovaries stop producing ripe eggs and menstruation ends. For men there is a slight decrease of fertility, or ability to father children, from the late teens on. But many men of seventy and older are still able to father children.

Question 12: Do people ever stop being able to have intercourse?
Answer: As long as they are in good health and have a mate, both men and women can continue to enjoy sexual intercourse.

Question 13: What does it mean to be homosexual?
Answer: Some men are sexually attracted to other men; some women are sexually attracted to other women; these people are homosexual, or gay. Adolescent boys and girls may go through a stage of being strongly attracted to others of their own sex, perhaps their own age, perhaps older, and then later develop attraction to the opposite sex. These young people are not homosexual and are simply going through a stage in their growth.

Many people feel an attraction for members of their own sex from time to time. If this is strong and continuous, such people are said to be homosexual. If it is rare, or if it never occurs, the people are said to be *heterosexual* (attracted to the opposite sex). If people continue to be attracted both to the same and to the opposite sex, they are called *bisexual*.

A person's sexual orientation is firmly set, probably in early childhood. Homosexuals may have a hard time because people discriminate against them socially and in jobs. However, there is growing understanding and acceptance of gay people in our society.

Question 14: What are some of the ways that a man and woman can use to avoid starting a baby when they have intercourse?

Answer: A baby will not be started unless a sperm and a live ripe egg join together. There are a number of reliable ways to prevent their joining, although none of them is foolproof, especially if they are not used carefully, intelligently, and exactly according to directions. One way to stop the sperm and egg from meeting is to block the path of the sperm. To do this, before a couple has intercourse the man may put a rubber cap, called a *condom,* over his penis, or the woman may put a different sort of cap, called a *diaphragm,* over the opening to her uterus.

Another way to avoid conception is for the woman to take pills or to have injections that stop eggs from ripening and coming out of her ovaries. Or a couple can simply avoid intercourse around the time they think the woman's ovaries are likely to produce a ripe egg. The woman may also place in her vagina, before intercourse, a chemical foam or jelly that kills the sperms before they can travel to meet the egg.

Yet another method of contraception is to have an object, called an *IUD* (*intrauterine device*), placed in the woman's uterus. The IUD prevents the egg from settling into the wall of the uterus. There is also a pill that will keep the egg from settling in.

It is possible for a man or a woman who does not wish ever to have any more children to be *sterilized*. To sterilize a man, a doctor ties and cuts the vas deferens so that no sperms can pass through (see Figure 5, page 28). To sterilize a woman, a doctor ties and cuts the fallopian tubes so that neither eggs nor sperms can pass (see Figure 2, page 23). Sterilization does not prevent a man or woman from enjoying sexual intercourse fully.

A couple is usually helped by their doctor to choose and use properly one of these ways of avoiding conception. Doctors and medical scientists are constantly seeking easier, less expensive, and even more effective methods of contraception.

These are just some of the questions you may wonder about. If you have other questions, or if there are other matters in this book that you want to know more about, ask your parents, teachers, or someone else to help you find the answers.

WHERE TO WRITE FOR
BOOKLETS ABOUT MENSTRUATION

ॐ

1. Educational Director
   Kimberly-Clark Corporation
   Neenah, Wisconsin 65956
   Ask for: *Very Personally Yours*
   and
   The Miracle of You

2. Educational Director
   Tampax Incorporated
   P.O. Box 7001
   5 Dakota Drive
   Lake Success, New York 11040
   Ask for: *Accent on You*

3. Consumer Information Center
   Box 6-GU
   Personal Products Company
   Milltown, New Jersey 08850
   Ask for: *Growing Up and Liking It*

INDEX

THE AUTHORS

CORINNE BENSON JOHNSON, born and raised in Massachusetts, received an A.B. in philosophy and was graduated Phi Beta Kappa from Smith College. After graduation, she taught at a girls' boarding school in Connecticut and then joined the *Harvard Business Review* as an editorial assistant. Since moving to Philadelphia she has held a variety of administrative jobs with the American Friends Service Committee, most recently in family planning and family life and population education, and as Director of programs in Latin America. She and her son, Ralph, live in Philadelphia.

ERIC W. JOHNSON has taught English for many years and has been involved with the sex education program at Germantown Friends School, Philadelphia, where he now serves as Clerk of the School Committee (Chairman of the Board). He was graduated Phi Beta Kappa, *magna cum laude,* from Harvard College and received his M.A. in teaching also from Harvard. Mr. Johnson has worked overseas with the American Friends Service Committee in Portugal, Morocco, Algeria, India, France, and Russia. The father of three children, he has alternately taught and worked with various Quaker programs. He speaks frequently on sex education, chiefly to teachers, school administrators, and parent groups, and acts as a school consultant.

Mr. Johnson is also the author of *Love and Sex in Plain Language, Sex: Telling It Straight, V.D., How to Live Through Junior High School,* and a number of English textbooks widely used in schools.